D0362686

why do **dogs drink** out of the **toilet?**

why do dogs drink out of the toilet?

101 of the Most Perplexing Questions Answered About Canine Conundrums, Medical Mysteries & Befuddling Behaviors

Marty Becker, DVM
Gina Spadafori

Health Communications, Inc.
Deerfield Beach, Florida

www.hcibooks.com

Cataloging-in-Publication Information is available through the Library of Congress.

©2006 Marty Becker and Gina Spadafori
ISBN 0-7573-0572-5

All rights reserved. Printed in the United States of America. No part of this publication may be reproduced, stored in a retrieval system or transmitted in any form or by any means, electronic, mechanical, photocopying, recording or otherwise without the written permission of the publisher.

HCI, its Logos and Marks are trademarks of Health Communications, Inc.

Publisher: Health Communications, Inc.
3201 S.W. 15th Street
Deerfield Beach, FL 33442–8190

Cover model Tucker Seidler, human owner ©Lana Seidler
Cover design by Larissa Hise Henoch
Inside book design by Lawna Patterson Oldfield

Contents

Foreword

From the day a new puppy comes home, we have questions. Mine came during that long first night, as I listened to Earl's heartbroken puppy whine. As he yipped for his mom and littermates, I wondered: Will my wife and I ever sleep again? Shortly after came the next question: How long will it take until he's housetrained?

Around 2 A.M., after his third walk, Earl finally fell asleep from exhaustion. But at 2:07 A.M., the mournful cries began again—until we finally gave in and let him sleep on a pillow between us. And then we asked ourselves another question: What were we thinking?

But by morning we took a look at his sweet and trusting puppy face and caught a whiff of his magical puppy breath, and we knew we had made the right decision. It truly was puppy love! The questions then become more practical: Why does he only throw up on the best carpet in the house? Why does he howl whenever we leave? What does he have against the mail carrier?

Before too long, we dog lovers are seeking to solve all the mysteries of the canine kingdom, such as, Why do dogs drink out of the toilet? Which is, of course, the title of this wonderful new book from a dream team: America's favorite veterinarian and his writing partner, who is also an award-winning pet care journalist. Dr. Marty Becker and Gina Spadafori obviously love animals, and they also love sharing the answers to all those questions we wonder about. The result is a book that's both educational and fantastically entertaining.

Settle down on the couch with this book and your dog. You'll both be happy you did.

Patrick McDonnell, *creator of "Mutts"*
www.muttscomics.com

Introduction

Dogs are not people.

Well, sure, you say, everyone knows that. Or do they? We talk to our dogs in our language as if they understand every word. We ask them questions, and answer those questions for them. We invite them to share our furniture, sleep on our beds, ride along with us when we run our errands. Who doesn't know someone who has cute outfits for a small dog—maybe even owner-dog matching outfits?

Dogs are not people, but we sure treat them that way. And that leads to a lot of questions and sometimes problems when dogs act like, well, dogs. Much of this behavior is unfathomable to us two-leggers, but it sure makes sense if you're a dog.

As people who share our knowledge of pets for a living (Marty as veterinarian, television and radio host, author, and internationally distributed columnist; Gina as an author and syndicated columnist), we are the lucky recipients of thousands of questions from pet lovers every year. Many we could answer in our sleep, while others are new or take an unusual twist on a common theme, causing us to pull out the stacks of reference books, rummage through our lists of professional contacts, and search the breadth and depth of Google.

But it's not just about answering questions. We love to laugh, and we know other people who share their lives with animals also have lively senses of humor. How could it not be true, with all the crazy things pets do? So we set out not only to write a book that's solidly grounded in the best information, but also one that will make you smile—and share that smile, and your love of pets, with someone else. Your dog, if no one else!

We love animals, and we love what they bring to our lives. We celebrate them with good cheer and the absolute best and most current of information as we offer this book to help you know your dog better.

So why do dogs drink out of toilets? Howl at sirens? Eat or roll in nasty stuff? The answers may surprise you, and we guarantee you'll find them interesting. Take a crash course in Canine 101, and you'll not only understand all dogs better when you're done, you'll also know your dog at a richer, deeper level.

Which means you'll be able to love your dog even more.

Dr. Marty Becker and Gina Spadafori

Q: Why do dogs drink out of the toilet? Is it safe to let them?

A: **We all have our likes and dislikes.** After all, champagne connoisseurs don't drink the bubbly from foam cups, and draft beer lovers think beer from an aluminum can is second-rate. While the very idea of drinking from a toilet disgusts us, our dogs have a different perspective.

Dogs consider the toilet an incredible, spring-fed porcelain fountain. From a dog's point of view, toilet water is better because it's fresher, cooler and hasn't been standing around in a little bowl for hours and hours. It's magically changed, refreshed, renewed with every push of the handle. The water stays cooler longer because of the porcelain container, and because the larger surface area of a toilet bowl leads to greater evaporation. And toilets are made of material that doesn't alter the taste of water the way metal or plastic can. (Not that toilet manufacturers think about such things, we're sure.) Greater oxygenation may also make the water "taste better." (Taste, of course, is always a very personal matter.)

Beyond these considerations, there may also be a built-in survival strategy at work. Toilets may satisfy a dog's instinct to choose running water. In nature, movement in the water breaks up the yeast, molds and contaminants that collect in stagnant pools. Given the choice, wouldn't you rather drink from a fresh mountain stream than a brackish pond? (Of course, these days the stream might be just as bad—but we're talking about a survival strategy that predates the modern age of industrial pollutants.)

Besides the allure of the water, there's the bathroom itself. Easy-to-clean floors made of tile or other smooth, cool surfaces make the bathroom one of the cooler rooms in the house—great for a dog nap on a warm day!

Still, experts recommend that dogs do not drink from the toilet, because the bowls may contain the residue of harmful cleaning chemicals and other unmentionables. Easy solution: Keep the lid down.

The K9 Water Company offers an assortment of vitamin-enriched water products for dogs with names such as Toilet Water (chicken flavor), Gutter Water (beef flavor), Puddle Water (liver flavor) and Hose Water (lamb flavor). We wonder who does the taste-testing. . .

Q: Why does my dog bark and pester me as soon as I get on the phone?

A: Anyone who has ever worked as a telemarketer can tell you that half the dogs in the world start barking the minute their owners get on the phone. Why? Because they've been taught to behave that way—accidentally.

The problem starts when a dog barks at you just once when you're on the phone. Maybe she wants your attention. Maybe she just felt like barking at that moment. If she did it while you were watching television or paying the bills, you'd probably ignore her. That means no reward for the behavior, which also means it's not likely to be repeated.

But if you're on the phone, you don't want the person on the other end to hear your dog barking—or to hear you yell at your dog to shut up. Chances are you'll pet your dog or throw her plush toy across the room just to keep her quiet. Before too long, you have a dog who starts yapping every time you pick up the phone, because that behavior has been rewarded.

Sometimes it even goes a step further. There are plenty of people who give their dog a treat to shut her up while they're on the phone. This is a big payoff for the dog, who is now rewarded for every yip with a cookie. Why would she stop barking? Dogs are not stupid.

The best way to avoid this problem is to prevent it: Don't reward your dog in the short term for behaviors you don't want in the long run. If she barks when you pick up the phone, ignore her. If that doesn't work, or if your dog is already a phone pest, ask your veterinarian for a referral to a dog trainer who can help you retrain her. Believe it or not, you *can* teach a dog to shut up on command.

Q: When dogs move their legs when they're sleeping, are they chasing things in their dreams?

A: **Dogs definitely remember things,** so it makes sense to believe they have the ability to dream, just as people do. After all, dreaming is a normal part of organizing and reorganizing memories.

Like humans, dogs have two kinds of sleep. The deeper kind is characterized by rapid eye movements, so it's known as REM sleep. We know humans dream during REM sleep. We also know the whining, heavy breathing, twitching and leg movements we've all seen in our dogs occurs during canine REM sleep. So it's not a far fetch to believe dogs are dreaming, too.

What are they dreaming about? We'll never know.

SAYINGS THAT DON'T WORK ANYMORE

On more that one occasion, I remember misbehaving and being sent to my room in our southern Idaho farmhouse to think things over. I also remember my older brother, Bobby, chortling with glee to anyone who'd listen, "Boy, Marty's in the doghouse now!"

Being "in the doghouse" meant you were in trouble. Big trouble. It meant you were, at least theoretically, tossed from the house, physically banished to the backyard and emotionally chained up.

But now that I have children and the opportunity to use the same phrase that's been seared into my consciousness (also onto my rear end, from a few swats!), I find that "being in the doghouse" has absolutely no meaning for my kids.

Why? Because they think of a doghouse not as some cramped, creepy, cold weekend project of a building tucked away in the backyard, but as our house. A combination house for both humans and dogs with four bedrooms, four baths, a wide-screen TV and a spa. And they're not alone in this: Go to any pet industry trade show and the booths hawking indoor beds for dogs far outnumber those selling outdoor doghouses.

When I was young, pets lived outside. Today, people and pets alike think of our house as a home for all.

My wife can't threaten to "treat me like a dog," either—another phrase I heard as a kid. I'd love to be treated like a dog at our house. It means hearing baby talk, being cuddled, tickled, tempted with treats, given the best spot on the couch, getting to sleep without interruption through the night and most of the day as well.

I wonder if our dogs think it's a "human-eat-human" world out there?

—Dr. Marty Becker

Q: Why are little dogs so keen to mix it up with big dogs?

A: **There's no doubt that many small dogs** have a big attitude, and some of them have a decidedly bad attitude. The blame rests with the people who own them, though, not with the diminutive ankle-biters themselves. Because they're so cute and so small, people often let these little dogs get away with everything.

Some small dogs react with bravado because they're afraid, but others really are trying to pick fights with bigger dogs. They're saying, "I'm a dog too! Want to make something of it?" These little bullies really believe they're as big and powerful as any other dog. And if they're allowed to bark at larger dogs from the safety of their own living room window, their tough-guy attitude can get worse over time. When the bigger dog passes by, the little one gets the idea that his big-dog bark sent the interloper packing. And that just puffs up his attitude a little more. Eventually, he comes to see himself as a Great Dane, and woe to any dog who crosses his path.

Many small dogs are constantly carried, which adds to the sense of elevated status. After all, it's easy to think you're a giant when you're so often looking down on the world.

It's all very cute, this little dog bluster, until a little dog runs up against a big dog who doesn't dig the attitude. The little dog may start the fight, but the big dog will always end it.

People who have small dogs must be sure they're not allowing or encouraging snotty behavior in their pets. Small dogs should be safely socialized with other dogs when they are young by attending puppy classes, and then should be well trained and protected. And don't let your little dog mix it up with a big dog. If your purse pup picks a fight, pick him up and go home.

Many little dogs are actually among the smartest of breeds, and you have to give some credit even to those who don't seem to have the highest IQs. After all, we all have to work for a living, but toy dogs? They have it ruff . . . er, rough. All the best food, cutest clothes, getting their hair and nails done, and being carried in designer bags into all the nicest stores—we should be so smart!

Q: Why do dogs insist on revisiting places where all the other dogs in the neighborhood pee?

A: **Because pee-mail is a big deal** to dogs. One decent whiff can tell you everything there is to know about every dog who has visited that spot. And when you're finished reading all the mail, it's only sociable to leave a message of your own.

Unneutered males, in particular, also feel the need to re-mark their own previous markings, because urine evaporates and the scent decays. A dog not only has to "repaint the signs" for his own satisfaction, but also because it tells the other dogs coming by who "owns" this territory and also how much time has passed since that individual last came this way. In territories dogs share—which is just about everywhere you might take your dog walking on a leash—everyone has to keep marking and re-marking to establish ownership.

Some dogs make more leg lifts than an aerobic instructor and have made a career out of marking every upright element on their walks, from the proverbial fire hydrant to every bush, tree and fence post. While it's only fair to let a dog take a couple of good sniffs and a leg lift here and there, it's bad manners on your part to let him stop at the front yard of every neighbor. A dog trainer can help you find the right compromise, so your dog sniffs and lifts a couple of times, but then keeps moving.

Q: Why does my dog take so long to poop?

A: *Who hasn't waited impatiently* in the worst of weather and for the dog to sniff, sniff, then sniff some more before dropping a load for all to see, smell or, unfortunately, sometimes step in. (Of course, we recommend that you stoop to scoop!)

While checking the "pee-mail" is an important form of communication for dogs, the deliberations involved in dropping the big loads doesn't seem to make as much sense—to us, at least. But feces are a much more visible territory marker than urine. A dog might well want to carefully evaluate the pros and cons of planting a fecal flag in some other dog's territory. Obviously, this is a decision that requires careful thought.

In some dogs, delaying is learned behavior. They've figured out that as soon as they're done, the outing's over—so they'll delay as long as possible. Give your dog a little extra walking time, perhaps with a fun game thrown in, and she won't feel it's so urgent to carefully schedule her poop.

Q: Is the whole Rockettes leg-lift thing really necessary?

A: **It is to a dog.** Better to put your scent mark at nose level, where other dogs can smell it and the breeze can more easily disseminate it. That's why dogs (mostly male, but even some females) contort themselves into precariously balanced tripods to get their urine-squirters into position to splash their pee as high as possible.

Of course, some males never really do get into it, especially if they're neutered. But the most precocious males start lifting a leg at four months of age.

For the most dedicated leg-lifters, the act can get pretty amusing when the dog is one of those small ones with a big attitude. While your average Irish Wolfhound can land the highest squirt with very little effort, if you're a bossy little Irish Terrier, you're going to have to try harder—a lot harder. Some small dogs get that hose up so high in an effort to top some taller dog's mark that they're practically doing a front-paw stand.

Q: When dogs yawn, are they sleepy or bored?

A: *Neither, really.* Think of yawning as a kind of switching gears. A yawn increases the flow of oxygen and boosts the heart rate—actions that give the brain a good goosing. A yawn can prepare the body for action—as in the yawning of a keynote speaker waiting for her introduction or a quarterback waiting to get back onto the field. Yawning can also be a way to relax.

Dogs yawn both to charge themselves up and to calm themselves down. It depends on the situation. If you go to a canine agility competition, you'll often spot dogs yawning at the starting line while waiting for the signal to explode across the line to the first obstacle. They're ready to run, and the yawn expresses that stress and excitement. In the waiting room of a veterinary hospital, you'll often see dogs yawning, too—a sure sign that they're stressed and trying to calm themselves.

In training classes, dog will often yawn—and owners will often interpret this as a sign that the dog is bored.

Not so. The dog who's yawning in obedience class is more likely stressed than bored, either from nervousness or from wanting to please you but not yet understanding how.

Just as in humans, yawning can be contagious in dogs. If you catch your dog's attention and yawn, you may well get a yawn back. Some experienced dog handlers actually use this to their advantage, encouraging their dogs to yawn as a way to get them either focused or relaxed.

Q: Why do dogs love to roll in stinky stuff?

A: *You know those sprays and plug-ins* you use to make the house smell fresh? Your dog is not impressed. If your dog were choosing a scent to make the house smell perfect, she might pick Old Dead Squirrel or Pile o' Cat Poop.

As much as we love our dogs, we have a difference of opinion when it comes to defining what smells "good." Considering that our dogs' sense of smell is hundreds of times better than ours, who's to say which species is right about what smells the best?

Now, about that rolling in those malodorous messes. It's pretty simple, actually: People like to put on nice scents, and so do dogs.

One theory on stink-rolling is that it represents a canine celebration of abundance. Now and then a dog will encounter a rewarding tidbit with a pungent smell; it's like a person finding a twenty-dollar bill on the ground. Sweet! It's certainly a good reason to stick a canine nose as close to the scent source as possible and inhale all that wonderful aroma. But to discover an entire rotting fish or other large pile of nastiness often triggers the urge to celebrate with a hearty roll; like a person who won the lottery throwing one-hundred-dollar bills all over the bed and "rolling in dough." You've noticed how silly-happy they look doing this, haven't you?

There's a survival element, too. For a hunting animal, there's a tactical advantage to not smelling like a predator: The prey don't know you're coming. Rolling in strong odors—feces and even dead animals—is thought to provide scent cover, to help predators land their lunch a little more easily.

Of course, none of our pet dogs have to hunt for their supper, but old instincts never really go away. That's why if there's a bad smell available, there's a good dog happy to roll in it. And not long after, a spoilsport human with warm water and soap ready to ruin it all—from the dog's point of view.

A cure for skunky dogs

Just about the worst thing any dog can smell like is skunk. In the interests of domestic bliss, we're going to share the best recipe ever for eliminating skunk smell.

Take 1 quart of 3-percent hydrogen peroxide, ¼ cup of baking soda (sodium bicarbonate, for you scientific types) and 1 teaspoon of liquid dishwashing soap, such as Ivory. Mix and immediately apply to the stinky pet. Rinse thoroughly with tap water.

You can double or triple the recipe if you have a big dog, but always get the solution on your pet as quickly as you can after you combine the ingredients. The chemical reaction is what eliminates the skunk smell, and it doesn't last long.

Don't mix up the solution in advance, and don't try to store it in a closed bottle—it'll burst any closed container you put it in. But do keep the ingredients on hand—just in case.

Commercial products are available that do a pretty good job, as well. And what about that old standby, tomato juice? Use it and what you'll end up with is a pink dog who still stinks—maybe just not quite as much.

Q: How strong is a really strong dog?

A: **Pretty strong.** According to the Saint Bernard Club of Alaska, on August 11, 1974, the Saint Bernard Kashwitna set a world record by pulling 6,000 pounds on wheels and won the title of World's Strongest Dog in the *Guinness Book of World Records*. His brother Susitna later set the world record, still unchallenged, for a weight pull on snow, by pulling 5,220 pounds at the 1976 World Championship Dog Weight Pull.

Q: Why do dogs hate it when you blow in their faces but love to hang their heads out of the car window?

A: *To a dog, the sensations of the wind* sweeping by at forty miles per hour and some two-legged primate blowing the smells of last night's dinner in the direction of her hypersensitive nose are not even remotely in the same category.

Compare your breath, even at its nicest, to the glorious smell-o-rama that is available to the dog who sticks her nose out the window of a moving car. For comparison, you might consider it the canine equivalent of our looking out the window of a high-speed train dashing through the loveliest part of the French countryside. While blowing in her face . . . well . . . that's like looking out a window into an air shaft with some trash cans at the bottom.

The rush of all kinds of scents is irresistible to an animal whose sense of smell is as complex and advanced as the dog's is. When we drive down the street, our puny noses can barely tell where the coffee shop is, and maybe the bakery. But our dogs can decode so much more from the air passing by when they're riding in a car, and the experience is surely pleasurable. That's why the characteristic expression of a dog with her head out the window is one of concentration and bliss—her mouth swept into a doggy grin that's better to get those scents to her nose and also to another scent organ, called the vomeronasal or Jacobson's organ, in the roof of the mouth. The more smells, the merrier, in the opinion of our dogs.

Not all canine pleasures are safe ones. That's why it's a good idea to keep the window rolled up and your dog's head inside the car. Road grit or an insect traveling at high speed can do a lot of damage to your dog's eyes. Or, no kidding, put dog goggles (Doggles) on them (they're used on military service and search-and-rescue dogs).

Q: Does tug-of-war teach a dog to be mean?

A: A few years ago, many dog trainers put tug-of-war on the list of games you should never play with your dog. The idea was that if you play tug-of-war and end it by giving the tug toy to your dog, you are letting the dog win a contest of strength against you. And that, the theory went, leads to dominant behavior.

While some trainers still aren't comfortable recommending the game, others believe you have to take it on a dog-by-dog basis. For a dog with aggression issues, it's probably not a good idea. But for a good-natured, well-socialized, well-trained family dog who knows the game is just . . . well, a game, it's probably fine. In fact, some trainers use tug-of-war as a reward or motivator after a strong performance in canine competitions.

Q: Do dogs really hate cats?

A: **Dogs chasing cats** was a staple of the cartoons we all watched when we were growing up. But one of the reasons we like dogs so much is that hate just doesn't seem to be part of their makeup. Do some dogs chase cats? Do some dogs kill cats? The answer is, unfortunately, "yes" in both cases. But the reason isn't because of some deep-seated cross-species animosity.

Cats occupy a fairly interesting ecological niche, right in the middle of the food chain: They are both predators and prey. Their skills as predators are obvious, but to many bigger predators—especially urban coyotes and some dogs—a cat pretty much looks like a tricky-to-catch but still tasty lunch. Some dogs are more into the prey thing than others, but for dogs who like to hunt for themselves, a cat is just another item on the menu. As the saying goes, "It's strictly business, nothing personal."

Behaviorists say that dogs who kill smaller animals or act aggressively toward other dogs are not necessarily a danger to humans. In fact, many are very reliable family pets. But they do need to be kept away from other animals. That means not just cats but also gerbils, ferrets, rabbits, birds, squirrels and anything else you don't want to find dangling from their mouths.

There are also dogs who will naturally chase anything that moves, from an animal to a bicyclist to a plastic bag blowing in the wind. These dogs will happily chase a cat and may even bite if they catch one, but would probably back off if the cat unsheathed her razor-sharp claws and promised to use them.

Finally, there are plenty of dogs who don't mind cats at all, and who even love the cats they know well.

While you can't say for certain which category any particular dog will fall into, you can make some general assumptions. Terriers, for example, were developed to be vermin killers, and many of these dogs have the detached professionalism of a gangland hit man when it comes to dispatching rodents such as mice, rats, and hamsters, and sometimes even smaller pets such as cats. Herding dogs, and sighthounds (dogs who hunt by visually sighting their prey) such as Greyhounds, probably are more interested in chasing than they are in killing a cat, but accidents do happen. Many sporting dogs, such as retrievers and spaniels, on the other hand, just don't see it as their job to pester the cat.

While some dogs can never be trusted around cats—their instincts and prey drive are just too strong—others can be socialized from a young age to at least tolerate cats and trained to leave them alone. If you have a cat and are thinking of adopting an adult dog from a shelter or rescue group, be sure to choose one who shows no signs of prey drive toward smaller animals.

Many animal shelters and rescue groups have a "test cat" who is relaxed enough to accept the short-term annoyance of being introduced to dogs, in the interest of gauging the canine's level of interest in cats.

Q: Why are some dogs terrified of thunderstorms?

A: **Some breeds and types of dogs** seem to be more high-strung and sensitive to noise, but the truth is that any dog can become terrified of storms. After all, a storm is more than just thunder: The atmospheric pressure changes, the sky lights up, static electricity builds and rain pounds on the roof. The smells in the air are so different that even we scent-challenged humans say, "Smells like rain." Imagine what an incoming storm smells like to our dogs!

For some dogs, fear of thunderstorms increases because their people mishandle the early signs of fear—either by soothing the dog or by punishing her. Soothing ("Poor baby! Don't be afraid. Come here and get a hug.") rewards the behavior; punishing makes a scary event even more frightening. Some dogs get so wound up that their fearful behavior becomes a reliable weather predictor for their owners, because dogs can sense a storm approaching long before we can.

Sensitivity to thunder is easier to prevent than to cure. When puppies and young dogs show concern, one strategy is to distract them. Give them something positive to do, such as starting a training session with lots of treats, or playing a favorite game. In other words, ignore the storm, distract the dog and set the tone by acting unconcerned. With a new dog, the first time there is a storm pretend it is an invitation to a "storm party." With every crack of thunder, respond, "Whoopee! That was a fun one, here's your storm cookie!" Couple this with happy requests for simple obedience commands, and the dog will soon look forward to storms.

Once a dog has developed a full-blown phobia, though, the fear of storms is quite dramatic—and can be dangerous. Some dogs may tremble, others may destroy their surroundings, and still others may bite out of fear.

If your dog is afraid of loud noises that you can predict—fireworks on holidays, for example—ask your veterinarian to prescribe a sedative for your pet just for those days.

For fearful dogs who live in areas that get a lot of thunderstorms, your best bet is asking your veterinarian for a referral to a behaviorist. A veterinary behaviorist will work with you on a treatment plan that may include medications, counterconditioning, pheromones and even antistatic jackets in an effort to help a dog to relax during storms.

Q: Do dogs get depressed?

A: **The emotional range of a dog** is not all that wide or deep, to be honest. That's one reason why a dog who seems to show what, in humans, might be signs of depression—lethargy, loss of appetite, changes in normal sleep patterns—is more likely to have a physical problem than a mental one.

Still, there's no denying that many dog lovers have observed what looks a lot like grief in pets who have lost a family member, either four-legged or two-legged. Perhaps the most well-known example of canine grief is that of Greyfriars Bobby, the Skye terrier who visited his owner's grave in Scotland every day for fourteen years, until the dog's own death in 1872. The fact that people noticed and rewarded the dog with food and shelter for his loyalty might have played a factor in his behavior, but we'd hate to ruin such a good story.

So, yes, it seems some dogs do have an emotional response to the loss of a beloved human or pet companion.

But dogs are also amazingly resilient when it comes to joining a new family. Think of shelter dogs. Can you imagine how much time people would have to spend in therapy if they were suddenly removed from one family and placed with another—in some cases, again and again? Although some newly adopted dogs go through an adjustment period that may include being anxious and destructive when left alone, most bounce back and become happy-go-lucky new family members.

"Love the one you're with," seems to be the motto of many a dog.

For people suffering from depression, studies show that one of the best treatment plans is to get a dog. The companionship, the responsibility and even the increase in activity required—because a dog must be walked—are all good for lifting people out of depression, or preventing it in the first place.

Q: When I leave my dog alone, he destroys things and makes a mess. Is he doing this out of spite?

A: **Spite and guilt are not part** of a dog's emotional repertoire. Dogs live in the here and now, and revenge is not in their gene pool.

As for barking, chewing and digging, well, they are natural, normal behaviors, part of every dog's DNA. Dogs who do that stuff are just being dogs. The fact that we'd rather these "job skills" never be trotted out in our homes is just a compatibility issue between canines and humans.

The motives people often attribute to dog behavior just aren't possible. Dogs have no idea a behavior is "bad" until you teach them in terms a canine can clearly understand. So they definitely don't chew because they're mad at you for leaving them; they chew because they're stressed about being alone and chewing is a canine stress reliever. As for the mess . . . well, sometimes a dog just can't hold it any longer. And the stress of separation can make that physical process more urgent.

"Aha!" you say (if you're the sort of person who says "aha!"). "If what you say is true, how come when I come home and find a mess, my dog looks guilty and tries to find a place to hide?" Why indeed?

But look at this situation again, through the dog's eyes. You're a dog, your owner comes home, and you're trotting happily down the hall to meet him when you hear . . . swearing. You pause, uncertain. Then . . . yelling, and you hear your name in the middle of that rant. And realize: He's angry at me! You have no idea why—you've long forgotten that you chewed up all his underwear or peed on the rug—but you're fairly certain the most prudent plan of action would be to take off.

When the guy finds you, he's so angry it scares you, and so you do your best to appease him, dog style. You roll over and show your belly, or maybe you squirt a little urine. A dog would see both efforts as a clear way of saying, "I'm sorry, I'm sorry. I don't know what's making you angry but I apologize, anyway." But instead . . . more yelling, and maybe a smack.

A display like this from you, even one time, doesn't teach your dog anything except that you're an unpredictable lunatic who cannot be appeased. Therefore, if you're a dog it's probably best to look humble and hide whenever the boss comes home.

Spite? Guilt? These are just too complicated for dogs, who tend to have a more simple range of emotions, like fear . . . and joy. Dogs are not drama queens. Their ability to live so simply and so joyfully is, after all, one of the reasons we love sharing our lives with them.

If your dog is making a mess of your home while you're gone, ask your veterinarian for a referral to a behaviorist who can help diagnose the symptoms of the problem and walk you through to a solution.

Q: Why is my dog so interested in airing my dirty laundry?

A: **Because it smells like you, of course!** What could be better than taking every piece of dirty laundry, the more intimate the better, and making a nice little nest out of it? Or chewing it up to release all those wonderful smells? Or bringing it out when your mother-in-law, minister or boss is over for dinner?

Some dogs love to share, after all, and the exciting chase games that often ensue are lots of fun, too. You don't agree? What a spoilsport!

The list of things dogs have chewed up because they've got their humans' scent on them would be longer than this book. Veterinarians, behaviorists and dog trainers have heard it all: Clothes (especially women's "been worn" undies with that "not so fresh smell" being the lotto winner), shoes (mmmm . . . leather!), remote controls and even Barbie dolls seem to be among the more popular items.

Easy solution: Put your things away! And offer your dog chewing alternatives, safe toys that will satiate that all-important desire to gnaw—especially among puppies who are teething and young adults who are still exploring the world with their mouths.

Q: How many teeth does a dog have?

A: **Puppies have twenty-eight teeth.** At around the age of four months, these so-called milk teeth start being pretty much replaced by forty-two permanent ones. Now and then, though, a dog will have an extra—a retained baby tooth.

A retained baby tooth can cause problems, including incorrect placement of permanent teeth, poor development of the jaw and infections. Fortunately, it's easy to fix. If you notice extra teeth, typically in the front, talk to your veterinarian, who can remove the extras and leave nothing but adult pearly whites behind.

Q: Why is it that you can't keep some dogs out of the ocean, lake or river, but have to drag them to the bathtub?

A: **Soap is likely one reason.** Another is being elevated and placed in a super-slippery container. A dog comes back from the beach completely stinky by human standards, but smelling just perfect by doggy ones. And what do we do? We throw her in the bathtub with soap. Soap that's scented for human noses, after all, not dog ones. When was the last time you saw a soap marketed with the aroma of Rotten Garbage or Stinky Fish?

Pet-care companies know animals don't pick out and—more important—don't pay for products, so they design them to appeal to humans. That means dog-cleaning products with scents like mint and citrus, neither of which would be in a dog's top 10 . . . or even top 100.

But bathing is more than a nasal assault. Combine fear of the unknown with restraint and slippery footing, then add in the sound of water crashing from the tap into the tub, and you've got a nightmare scenario to some dogs. Of course, many dog lovers know it's better to fill the tub behind closed doors before adding the dog, and to place a mat in the tub to improve footing. But still . . . it's a bath, and that makes it Evil in the doggy dictionary.

You can ease bathophobia by changing the way your dog feels about the bathtub. Try feeding the dog in a dry tub or giving them an irresistible treat (piece of hot dog), so she associates positive activities with that location. Since she is unlikely to jump in at first, begin feeding her in or near the bathroom, and move about a foot closer each day. Once the dog is jumping into the dry tub, add just a little water and offer some outrageously delicious treats as a reward for wading. Work up to more water, a little at a time.

Skip the scented shampoo, too. The best shampoo smells like nothing at all. And don't forget the special goodie at the end of every bath, like a kid getting a lollipop for being good during a haircut, and soon your dog will look forward to bath time. Especially if you're careful not to get any soap in her eyes!

Forget that old nonsense about how a dog shouldn't be bathed more than every six months or even once a year. That might have been okay for farm dogs, but honestly, would you want to live with an animal bathed that infrequently? How often is appropriate? As often as necessary to make your dog huggable, one you don't mind sharing a bed with. And remember, even weekly bathing isn't necessarily a bad thing. Ever see a dog show? Those dogs are washed and slathered with conditioner every single week—and sometimes even more often. Their coats look great!

Q: Why must a dog shake like a washing machine on the spin cycle, then zoom around the room after every bath?

A: **Shaking is a canine reflex.** The weight of the water in a saturated coat doesn't feel right, and something is triggered deep in the doggy brain. A healthy fur coat is a dog's best protection from the elements, and if the coat is completely saturated, it's not going to do its job.

Hence, the big shake—the closer in proximity to perfectly dry humans, the better. (We just made that last part up; there's no scientific evidence that dogs prefer to shake all over the driest, most dog-disliking human within range. It just seems that way.) Dogs will generally start from the head and shake from front to back, and will shake when the fur around their head, neck and shoulders is wet but possibly not when just their hind ends or feet are. Taking a trick from professional groomers, if you want to prevent your dog from shaking—for example, you need to reach over and get a towel—just hold their nose in your hand; if they can't move their head, they can't start shaking.

As for the postbath zoomies, there are a couple of explanations. One is that the dog is so happy to be out of the bathtub and your iron grip that he bounces off the walls. Or maybe it's because a dog feels better clean than he did dirty. But maybe not. Because many dogs immediately throw themselves in dirt, piles of leaves or even manure, and that's probably about covering up the nasty—to a dog—smell of pet shampoo with something more acceptable. Honestly, you can't expect a dog to greet other dogs smelling like Ruff-Ruff Rosemary or Pet-astic Peppermint, can you? What will his buddies think?

Q: Why do dogs get car sick?

A: **Don't worry, it's not your driving skills.** Dogs aren't designed to ride in cars—any more than we are—and the experience can be physically and emotionally unsettling, especially for young dogs. The motion of the vehicle can affect the inner ear, triggering nausea and dizziness.

Other dogs become upset in the car because they've learned it's not an experience that ends well. If car rides are infrequent and end at a destination that is not exactly a dog's favorite—such as the groomer or the veterinarian for the trimming of nails or something far worse (the family jewels)—a dog's dislike of the car may be difficult to overcome.

Many dogs, like many kids, outgrow the car sickness they experience as puppies, become accustomed to the sensation of motion and learn that car rides are fun. For those dogs who aren't accepting the idea that cars are great, changing the animal's attitude is the answer.

To slowly condition a puppy or dog to think of the car as fun, start simply by offering her treats in the parked car and calling it a day—without even starting the engine. After treats, try feeding her a normal meal on the car floor. Next, try short trips to nowhere, with lots of praise and treats. Build up to longer rides. If the destination is a good one—a puppy socialization class, the park or a dog biscuit at the drive-through bank window—you may find your pet becomes an easy rider before you know it.

Play it safe, though. Driving with your dog loose in the car is risky both for your dog and your ability to concentrate on the road. Your dog should be secured in a crate or with a canine seat belt. In an accident, a canine projectile can make things worse, for dogs and people both.

Doubt us? Ask bestselling author Stephen King, who in a real-life nightmare was almost killed when he was hit by a man trying to deal with his loose dog while driving down the road.

When dogs have upset stomachs for any reason, they drool. In some dogs this is the only sign of car sickness, and in other dogs it is the precursor to vomiting.

Q: Why do dogs cock their heads when they hear unusual sounds?

A: **Because it's cute, of course.** Well, not really. A dog will tip his head to bring one ear forward, so he can better focus on the source of an unusual sound, or a favorite one ("Cookie?"). Typically, these unusual sounds are high-pitched noises, such as squeaks. That makes sense, when you consider that many dogs will happily catch a rodent if the situation presents itself.

We humans love this reaction, which is no doubt why we put squeakers in so many dog toys—and why so many dogs love these toys.

Puppies are more likely to tip their heads frequently, because to them, all sounds are new. As a dog ages, you might get an ear flip rather than a full head tilt. Hey, they've heard it all before.

Q: Why do dogs jump up to greet people?

A: **From a dog's point of view,** a better question is, "Why don't humans walk on all fours like just about every other animal and meet me at my level?"

When dogs greet each other, they check out the places where the scent is strongest—the mouth, the genitals and the anal area—the latter being home to some potent scent-producing glands. That's why dogs greet each other with a peck on the cheek and we're not talking about the ones on your face. This behavior makes perfect sense for an animal as smell-driven as the dog, even if mouth-licking and crotch-sniffing are not considered polite behavior in human society. An untrained dog will try to connect instinctively, and that means starting the greeting by jumping up for a closer whiff of human breath—followed by a dive for the crotch.

Dogs have to be trained in human etiquette, and a lot of times we don't do a good job of it. We may, for example, have rules that make perfect sense to us but are completely incomprehensible to a dog. Do you let your dog jump up on you when you're in jeans but yell at her for doing the same when you're dressed for an evening out? Congratulations! You've just failed the dog logic test.

Maybe it's not really your fault, though. Every dog owner has dog-loving friends who walk in patting their chests to get a paws-up greeting. How is a dog to understand that jumping up is okay with some people but off-limits with others? Likewise, many people let little dogs jump up because it's cute and easier than bending down to greet the dog. And little dogs quickly learn this behavior will get them picked up.

Pick a set of rules—dog rules, people rules or some combination of the two. But whichever rules you pick, be consistent and don't expect your dog to magically understand when jumping up is okay and when it isn't. It's either okay all the time, or it's forbidden.

Q: Why do some dogs squat and pee when they meet people?

A: *Don't you just love the fact* that another mammalian species is so excited to greet you that it just loses bladder control? Probably not. Puddlus Unexpectous (we made this up) is completely different behavior from the canine delinquent who lifts his leg on a visitor. The dog who offers a puddle as a greeting is far from the obnoxious top-dog wannabe the leg-lifter is.

A dog who piddles his salutations isn't exhibiting a housetraining lapse or making a statement of assertiveness, but rather is offering what's known as submissive urination. This behavior is relatively common in young, shy, sweet-natured dogs. It typically occurs when the dog is greeting a guest or a returning family member, but it can also happen when a dog is being scolded.

A lot of dogs are punished for peeing when their humans come home, and that's neither fair nor helpful.

Dogs and wolves use submissive urination to reinforce pack order: An immature or low-ranking animal will roll over and squirt urine to acknowledge the higher rank of a more dominant pack member. In a way, your dog is paying you a compliment, saying, in effect, "You're the boss, and I'm acknowledging that." That, plus, "Oh, by the way, please don't hurt me!"

Physical and emotional maturity—in your dog, that is—will often help with this problem, but you can't rely on time to do the whole job. Dogs who urinate in greeting need to have their confidence and trust boosted—and they need a visit to the veterinarian to make sure there's no physical problem contributing to the behavior.

With a puddler, delay the greeting for several seconds until the dog is a little calmer. Present a less-threatening posture by crouching with your side facing him, rather than coming at the dog head-on. Allow him to approach you rather than coming straight toward him, and speak softly.

Because some dogs are frightened by a hand coming down on them from above, pet your dog under the chin instead of on top of the head, and don't make direct eye contact, which can also be intimidating to a shy dog.

Once you determine what type of greetings result in a urine-free response, you can build on your success and your dog's confidence by gradually adding enthusiasm to your greetings.

What's the best way to build a dog's confidence? Train him! Training offers a dog chances to be successful and to please you. It teaches him to think and work out problems, and to look to you for cues about how to behave.

Q: Why do some dogs insist on snacking from the cat's litter box?

A: **As incredible as it seems to us,** many dogs consider cat feces to be every bit as delicious as dog biscuits. It's the extra protein, and it smells as delicious to many dogs as fresh baked cinnamon rolls or fresh popped popcorn does to us humans. (Cat food has a higher level of protein than dog food, which is also why many dogs also prefer the undigested kitty rations to dog food.)

When faced with easy access to a constant supply of kitty "snacks" in a handy serving tray, few dogs can resist for long—which is why efforts to train a dog to leave the litter box alone are not often successful.

The better plan is to restrict the dog's access, which you can accomplish in many ways. Here are a few suggestions:

- **Get covered litter boxes.** Some cats don't like them, and cats with asthma can't use them. If your cat falls into either category, this solution isn't going to work for you.

- **Change the litter box location.** Of course, you must be careful not to upset your cat. But you can experiment by gradually moving the litter box to a location that is too high for the dog to reach.
- **Provide barriers.** One way is to rig the door to the room containing the litter box so that it stays open wide enough for the cat but not for the dog. Another possibility is to put a cat-sized hole in the door to the litter box room if your dog is medium or larger. For small dogs, try blocking off the room with a baby gate; the cat can easily jump over it, but the dog can't.

Don't forget to scoop the litter box several times a day. A dog can't eat what a dog can't find.

Q: What's the easiest, neatest way to pick up after my dog?

A: No small number of entrepreneurs have come up with variations on devices designed to pick up after a pooch. Some of these are quite clever, and they all work just fine. But perhaps the easiest—and certainly the cheapest—is a plastic grocery bag. Put it over your hand like a glove, grab the mess, flip the bag inside-out over it, tie the handles and dispose of appropriately.

Your neighbors will thank you for your consideration, believe us!

Q: Are some dogs gay? I've seen male dogs humping other males. I've seen females humping other females—or even males. Neutered dogs, too. What's that about?

A: Humping isn't just about procreation—it can also be about dominance. When an intact male ("intact" is veterinary speak for "still has his testicles") does the mating dance with an unspayed female in season, that is all about procreation, and puppies are nature's intended result.

But when you see all the other possible combinations, even in neutered dogs—male on male, female on male, what have you—one dog is telling the other who claims top ranking. You can even see these messages being sent among relatively young puppies, who will often hump their littermates—just as frequently on the front end as the back. Practice makes perfect!

ARE DOGS GOOD IN BED?

Let me set the bedtime scene: We live in a log house nestled in the pine trees halfway up mile-high Hall Mountain in northern Idaho. Our king-size bed has one of those cushy, pillow-top mattresses covered with flannel sheets and a goose down comforter that's six inches thick when fluffed. At night, when we get ready for bed, we crack open a window to let in the pine-scented night air and the soothing sounds of the crickets and toads that serenade our pending slumber.

On opposite sides of the bed, my wife and I fluff our respective feather pillows, lift up the comforter and get comfortable as we prepare to sleep nose to nose with our respective partners. Four-legged, hairy partners that is, with more than a hint of doggy breath.

Many things have changed in our almost thirty years of marriage. In the early years, I was like a tomcat possessed, always on the prowl for a little loving. My wife, Teresa, was receptive more often than not, and she loved to kiss, nuzzle and cuddle.

Then we got pets, and our love life took a backseat to rituals involving the other critters in our bed. In the early years, Teresa would dress seductively for me, in something as transparent as cellophane. Now, because she wants to keep Quixote the Papillion-Poodle-Yorkie cross warm, she wears pajamas that make body armor seem delicate.

After we each settle in with our respective partners—Teresa with Quixote and myself with the hairy princess, Scooter, an aging Wirehaired Fox Terrier—we stay on our respective sides of the bed, engaging in four-play rather than foreplay.

Personal comfort was everything in the early years of marriage, as we spooned, sprawled out, and rotated, seeking the softest, warmest spot on the bed. Now we let the pets decide first where they want to sleep, then position ourselves around them in semiparalytic states. We dare not move to relieve a cramp or pull up the comforter, lest we fail to "let sleeping dogs lie."

Speaking of pet positions in bed, whatever happened to those images of dogs curled up at the foot of the bed, nose to tail, in a compact, contented crescent of fur? Pets seem to have lost this ability; now they sprawl out, making themselves as long as possible with their lolling tongues hanging out one end and their tails beating like a slow metronome on the other. In the Becker house, we have a name for it: furban sprawl.

During the night it goes from bad to worse. Now that I'm over forty, my prostrate and bladder (P&B) are cohorts in making sure I don't sleep the night without visiting the porcelain throne. My P&B persist, but I resist, because I know that if I get up to go to the bathroom, Quixote, Scooter or both will move over to occupy the warm depression I leave behind, without the least bit of hesitation or guilt.

We still have the same alarm clock we got as a wedding present. Although it's old, it's almost in mint condition, since we don't use it. Why? Because we have dogs who wake us up, like clockwork, because they're hungry, thirsty, need to do their business or sense imaginary movement outside the bedroom.

In the morning, the dogs rise fully rested after having slept eighteen of the last twenty-four hours, while Teresa and I get ready to drag ourselves out of bed with chronic sleep deprivation. But as Quixote and Scooter lick our faces, delight us with their antics and wiggle with delight, we smile "the smile"—the one only pet lovers can appreciate. We wouldn't have it any other way.

—Dr. Marty Becker

Q: If a purebred dog mates with a mutt and has puppies, are future litters from the purebred dog going to be mutts, too?

A: **Mutts, Heinz 57, canine cocktails,** whatever you call them you've got to love the fact that dogs are such a plastic species with every make and model imaginable. With so many unwanted dogs in this country, it's sometimes very tempting for veterinarians and other pet experts to tell the person whose purebred dog just had a "whoops" litter that such a thing is true; that every subsequent litter after the one with the "mystery dad" will be more mixed-breed puppies. So, please, can we go ahead and schedule that spay for your dog, ma'am?

Honesty is the best policy, though, which is why we feel compelled to admit that if your purebred Golden Retriever delivered a litter of spotted, short-legged puppies who look a bit like the neighbor's rangy mutt, it's not all over. If you breed her to a purebred Golden Retriever next time, the puppies will be purebred Goldens. Each canine liaison is an individual event.

Of course, we're hoping you spay her anyway, unless you really want to increase her risk of developing cancer or any one of the several deadly infections that can kill unsprayed dogs. Or unless you're interested in being a reputable breeder, which means paying big bucks to make sure your girl is certified clear of hereditary defects such as eye disorders and hip dysplasia. And then spending the first eight weeks making sure the puppies are properly socialized to make good pets.

So, if you were hoping to turn a tidy profit on the family pet by selling purebred Golden Retriever puppies, but your dog had other ideas when she came into season, then promise us you'll socialize and then find great homes for those mixed-breed puppies. And then consider spaying her, to prevent future accidental matings—or even planned ones.

She'll be healthier, and you'll be happier without the problems that come with keeping her from the boys in the 'hood when she's next in season.

Q: Is it possible for the puppies in the same litter to have different fathers?

A: Obviously, all the puppies will have the same mom, but puppies in the same litter can have different dads. That can happen naturally, if a female dog in season gets out and finds more than one willing male (and like bar patrons near closing time, just about all intact male dogs are willing all the time). But it can also happen intentionally.

Reputable breeders don't overbreed their females, since they know it's not healthy for a dog to be used year after year as a puppy-making machine. But if you have a top champion female and you're looking at her limited ability to pass along her genes, you may, as a breeder, consider mating her to not one certified fabulous stud dog, but two. The daddy dog doesn't even have to be present, thanks to artificial insemination.

How does it all get sorted out as far as pedigrees are concerned? More modern technology: DNA testing.

These technological advances are not without controversy. In some rare breeds, litters with several sires are considered a way to increase genetic diversity in a dangerously small gene pool. But a lot of traditionalists think artificial insemination and multi-sired litters are changes that simply aren't needed in a system of dog breeding that has been going along just fine for hundreds of years without modern technology.

It didn't take long for some sharp operator to figure out another use for canine DNA tests. Once upon a time, you couldn't prove the neighbor's mutt jumped the fence and mated with your top champion female, no matter how much her puppies looked like him. But now you can. Yes, there have been a smattering of "puppernity" suits, and there are likely to be more.

Q: Will a male dog mate with his mother, or a female with her dad? Don't they know that's wrong?

A: Human ideas of morality don't matter to dogs.

This is what the female dog knows: "I'm in season. I need to be bred. He has what I need. C'mere, big guy. . . ." People sometimes think the male dog is the only one interested in mating (think college sophomore at a fraternity party), but a female dog in season is perfectly capable of working very hard to get herself bred (once again, college sophomore at a fraternity party—girls go to them, too). A dog in heat may even back up to a chain-link fence, crouch to allow smaller suitors access or even work neutered males into such a froth that they'll attempt intercourse, sometimes successfully—albeit without the possibility of puppies.

This is what the male dog knows: "She's in season. Ohhhhhhhhhh bay-beeeeee!"

Many a pet owner who has raised a mixed-gender pair of puppies together, or kept a puppy from a previous litter as a companion to a parent, has been surprised to find sis, mom, or daughter turn up preggers. Oops! Desperation is the mother of . . . well, never mind.

Bottom line: No matter how closely related, dogs will breed if they can. It's all about hormones. They don't know or care that in human society, such matings aren't acceptable.

Q: Why do dogs get stuck together and face away from each other after mating?

A: **In the old days,** before widespread spaying and neutering—as well as strong leash laws—canine Romeos roamed far and wide looking for the proverbial bitch in heat. When they caught a whiff of her in the air, there wasn't much that could keep them from their appointed task: to hook up, literally.

Many children got their first birds-and-bees lesson not on the Internet (as it seems most do now), but by watching neighborhood dogs mating. What they saw was that after mating, dogs stay stuck together and even turn around so as not to look at each other anymore. After-sex snuggling? No thanks!

To today's urban pet owner, the position past generations of pooch-watchers saw all the time seems improbable, even downright uncomfortable. But to dogs, of course, it all makes sense.

Let's start with the mechanics: The dog's penis, typically hidden inside a protective sleeve called the prepuce, or sheath, protrudes when it becomes erect. The penis base swells during copulation like the bulb on a turkey baster; its job is to lock the penis inside the female. After mating, the female's muscles contract around the bulb of the male's penis, and the canine Cupids become what is referred to as "locked" or "tied" for anywhere from 30 to 60 minutes.

The "tie" prevents the semen from escaping and increases the chance the female will become pregnant. While waiting, the male will turn around to face away from the female. It's easier on the male, who was supporting his weight on his back legs, and on the female, who was supporting the weight of them both.

Forcing them apart during this natural phase will likely injure one or both dogs. If the two haven't separated in an hour, experts recommend putting down the garden hose and instead, pushing down on the male's rump to help "untie Cupid's knot," or putting an ice pack on the male's testicles. Oooch!

SHE'S GOTTA HAVE IT

In my life, about half my pets have been rescued animals and half not. The ones who joined my family with fancy pedigrees were chosen because one of my hobbies is competing with my retrievers in various canine sports, including dog shows.

Heather was my first show dog, a Flat-Coated Retriever from the best lines in the breed. While she was competing for her conformation championship, I had to put off spaying her. Dog shows, you see, are supposed to be about evaluating breeding stock, and if a dog is altered the possibility of breeding is definitely out. That's why you see judges slipping their hands between the legs of male dogs to count testicles. Fewer than two will get you disqualified. It looks weird, but it's a dog show.

Along with Heather, I had another Flat-Coated Retriever by the name of Ben. Ben joined my home after a brief career as a blood donor in a veterinary hospital—a noble profession, but not one you'd choose for life. Ben was neutered, and his affection for Heather was nothing more than platonic—at first.

Like many people, I had always assumed that when it came to doggie sex, most of the pursuing was done by the males. After all, aren't they the ones who are always digging under or jumping over fences to follow their noses to a willing female? Well, maybe, but some females do everything they can to make mating possible, and Heather was that kind of a girl.

When she was in season, she pestered neutered Ben without mercy, backing her fanny into his face time and time again. The poor boy didn't really understand what she wanted, didn't know how to help, and just stood there, a look of canine confusion on his face. Exasperated, Heather would look back and below as if to say, "I know you have what I need . . . use it!"

This went on twice a year for three years, with Heather frustrated and Ben confused. It was a relief to us all when Heather wrapped up her show career and I made the appointment for her to be spayed.

Ben never said so, of course, but I'm sure he was grateful.

—Gina Spadafori

Q: Can a grown dog recognize her mother or a littermate if she meets them again?

A: **No one can say for sure,** but many a longtime reputable breeder has noted that dogs not only seem to recognize others of their breed, but also seem to have some natural affinity for close relatives. And that makes some sense. After all, the brains of puppies are completely wired by eight weeks of age, so they may retain a memory of their family members.

That doesn't mean they'll always be happy to see them again, though. As we humans know only too well, family relationships can be pretty complex.

Q: Why is it that when some male dogs go in for neutering, it turns into exploratory surgery?

A: It's normal for humans to feel a little sorry for the family dog who happily jumps in the car for a ride, only to discover that the trip is nothing less than a heinous plot arranged between his owners and the nasty veterinarian to remove his family jewels. Every male, of every species, let out a collective moan here.

In fact, neutering is one of the easiest and most routine procedures any veterinarian will do. But sometimes things turn out to be a little more complex than expected. In some dogs, all that ought to be there isn't; one or both of the testicles haven't descended from the abdomen into the cooler climate of the scrotum. Which is why sometimes veterinarians have to go hunting, so to speak.

If you are the kind of person who will bet on anything:

- Unilateral cryptorchidism (one hung low) is three times more common than bilateral cryptorchidism (two no-show).

- The right testicle is retained twice as often as its left bedfellow.
- Male dogs are 100 percent more affected with retained testicles than female dogs. (Okay, we just threw that in to make sure you were still paying attention.)

Surgical relocation of retained testis to the scrotum is considered unethical, so the veterinarian will remove the low-hanging fruit, then do an exploratory surgery to find and remove the wayward nut.

The tendency to retain testicles is genetic and is most commonly found in Toy Poodles, Yorkshire Terriers and Pomeranians. Reputable breeders remove such individuals from the breeding pool by having them neutered.

Q: Do female dogs have "biological clocks"?

A: **Dogs don't form support groups** to lament their inability or lost opportunities to reproduce, but false pregnancies are not uncommon in unspayed dogs. The reasons for them are hormonal, though, not emotional.

The signs of false pregnancy include nesting, mothering objects such as a stuffed animal and excreting milk. Some dogs may physically appear pregnant and may even go into labor. These symptoms become noticeable three to six months after a heat, and are caused by an abnormality in the hormonal cycle.

If symptoms are mild, the condition will usually resolve itself within three weeks. It may be tempting to put warm compresses on the dog's underside or to wrap the abdomen to prevent milk leakage in the house. But that's not advised, since any stimulation of the dog's mammary tissues encourages more milk production.

Continued or severe symptoms will require your veterinarian's assistance. After the false pregnancy has passed, the dog can be safely spayed, preventing future false pregnancies—and, of course, real ones as well.

Once spayed, we can assure you that your dog won't miss for a minute the puppies she never had.

Q: Is it really safe to spay and neuter young puppies?

A: It used to be that six months was considered the best age at which to spay or neuter a dog. But veterinary organizations long ago put their seal of approval on spaying and neutering puppies (and kittens) as young as eight weeks old. The reason for the change? Many people who left shelters with puppies, promising to spay or neuter them later, eventually returned with more puppies. And that didn't do anything to help reduce pet overpopulation.

While many shelters and humane societies now practice early spay/neuter, it's still fine to wait until your puppy is older—up to the more traditional six months.

Spaying a female will protect her from potentially deadly cancers and infections. The health benefits of neutering a male aren't quite so obvious (although there is some evidence that it reduces the incidence of prostate problems, and it certainly prevents testicular tumors), but the behavioral advantages are huge. Neutered males are less likely to fight, mark territory or roam.

Talk to your veterinarian about the advantages and the timing. It's a good idea, no matter what your puppy or dog's age.

Q: Why do dogs like to have their ears and tummies rubbed?

A: When it comes to feeling good, what could feel better to our dogs than a good old belly rub or back-of-the-ear scratch? But there is a twist or two on the real reason dogs like their ears and bellies rubbed.

Ears first. Dogs probably like their ears rubbed because, neurologically speaking, gentle massage in these areas is relaxing. The vagus nerve serves a large part of the midportion of the ear, and stimulating this nerve is calming because it controls vegetative, restorative (let's call it what it is—couch potato) functions. This calming effect also counteracts the fight-flight response associated with the sympathetic nervous system.

That's a mouthful of an explanation, but it simply means ear-scratching puts our pooches into "the zone." An ear scratch can help send a Type A pooch into yoga meditation.

Ear-licking might as well be considered foreplay by our four-legged friends. This courtship behavior is typically something the male does to the female. When one dog is constantly licking the ear of another, though, give a look and a sniff inside the ear. Ear infections produce excess ear wax or pus, and both of these may tickle the taste buds of other dogs. (Yuk!) So before assuming it is all foreplay, be sure the ear canals are healthy, pink and sweet smelling.

Now for tummy rubs. Rubbing in any area redirects blood to the area and relaxes tension. It's also thought that by exposing the area with the least amount of hair, dogs can cool off by going belly up and catching the breeze.

For dogs, rolling over and exposing one's belly can also be a submissive gesture. Maybe tummy rubbing starts with our dog bowing in respect to our authority, and it doesn't end there. Once you begin to tickle, lightly scratch or rub an exposed dog belly, the dog quickly learns to roll over more often to get that doggy-delicious experience.

Q: When you hit just the right spot on a dog's tummy, side or rump, why does he pump his leg?

A: You can blame it on fleas, as many people do. But even a flea-free dog has a reflex reaction to any passing skin irritation, whether it's an insect crawling between his hairs or a fingernail giving a scratch. If nerve endings detect something tickling the skin, the dog's leg will automatically come up to scratch the pest off—even if there's no pest there.

The response is most pronounced if you scratch a dog on the rump near the base of the tail, along the upper part of the flanks or on the belly—places where fleas like to congregate. Your dog knows you're doing the scratching for him, but he just can't help moving that leg.

The leg-pumping "scratch reflex" is so predictable that veterinarians will use it to help with their neurological exam when spinal damage is suspected.

Q: Why do some dogs hump their toys?

A: Same reason guys scratch their, well, you know. Because it feels good. Unneutered adolescent males are probably most interested in the behavior, with stuffed animals being likely targets.

Neutering reduces sex drive—along with aggression, urine marking and wanderlust—but doesn't necessarily stop a dog from pursuing a, shall we say, very close relationship with a favorite stuffed animal or pillow.

What about when dogs lick themselves? An old saying comes to mind: "Why do dogs lick themselves? Because they can!" There's a certain amount of truth to that. While the behavior is partly about keeping everything clean, it's pretty certain dogs also lick themselves because the sensation is a pleasant one.

Because there's also the possibility of a medical problem with a dog who seems obsessed with his privates, you ought to have your veterinarian take a look-see.

Q: Why do dogs eat grass when it seems to make them throw up?

A: One theory goes that eating and vomiting grass has evolutionary benefits. If the wild canid took a chance and ate something she shouldn't have, it likely caused nausea. This triggered an instinct to eat more grass than usual. This extra grass served two functions. First, it intertwined with the offending material. Then it irritated the lining of the stomach, resulting in both the grass and the bad stuff being regurgitated. Nowadays, so the theory goes, all dogs tend to eat grass when they're nauseous, even if the cause of the nausea is not a dietary indiscretion.

Another theory holds that dogs eat grass because it tastes good and/or fulfills a nutritional need for fiber and chlorophyll, both of which assist in digestion. This explains why dogs will commonly eat small amounts of grass without vomiting.

The truth is, no one really knows for sure why dogs eat grass. But there's no reason to stop them from doing so, in moderation.

Q: Is it fair to blame the dog every time you smell something bad?

A: As comedian Jeff Foxworthy says, "If the dog passes gas and you claim it . . . you might be a redneck!"

Besides being a running joke that's stood the test of time, dogs are an obvious choice to blame when someone gets a whiff of what's wafting up from under the table. You couldn't really blame Grandma or the goldfish, could you?

So what's up with the smell? Odorless gasses (nitrogen, oxygen, hydrogen, carbon dioxide and methane) make up 99 percent of the intestinal gas of pets (and people). The characteristic unpleasant, noxious odor comes primarily from trace amounts of volatile sulfur compounds, such as hydrogen sulfide.

Four-legged gas-passing (the scientific name for farting is "flatus") is most commonly caused by bacterial fermentation in the large colon of foods that contain a lot of fiber, poorly digestible protein, or foods such as soybeans or beans that contain large amounts of nonabsorbable oligosaccharides (sugars). The Mastiff musical-fruit category includes apples, grapes, prunes, raisins and bananas.

Many dogs do not digest dairy products easily, either. If you feed your lactose-intolerant dog excessive amounts of lactose-containing foods, such as cheese, milk and ice cream, the end result is Got Milk = Got Gas.

To put a cork in your pet's pressure problem, your veterinarian may have you take steps to decrease the amount of air your dog swallows as she eats and make some dietary changes that decrease her fiber intake. The vet may also ask you to walk your dog outside after she eats, where exercise can clear her colon and a little breeze can go a long way toward clearing the air.

You have to give credit to any inventor who spends their time coming up with products to reduce the smell of dog farts. And would you believe a few such products exist? First, there is a Bean-o type product for dogs, called CurTail, that works from within to keep odors down. More recently, there's The Doggone, a canine thong with an activated charcoal insert to trap the odors. Amazing, isn't it?

Q: Is it better to feed a dog once or twice a day, or just leave food out and let him eat whenever he wants?

A: **There are some dogs** who know when enough is enough at an all-you-can-eat buffet. And there's no doubt that just keeping the food dish full is an easy way to go for pet owners.

But it seems that our dogs have as much trouble pushing back from the proverbial table as we do. More than 40 percent of adult dogs ages five to 11 are overweight, or worse, obese. Those kinds of numbers have experts suggesting that dog food should be measured, not left out to be eaten in whatever amount your chowhound prefers.

Aside from the nutritional aspects, there are many behavioral advantages and some other health ones to controlling your dog's food dish. Teaching a puppy to sit using the food dish is as easy a pie: Just hold the dish over the puppy's head and say "sit." The little one will lose his balance, his butt will hit the ground and . . . voila! The food you give him rewards the behavior. You can expand on this by using meals to help train other commands, too, including "down," "stand" and "stay." Your dog will be exceptionally motivated, which makes the job easier.

As for whether to feed once or twice a day . . . the jury's still out on that one. Many people prefer dividing the day's ration into two portions, perhaps because it feels like the right thing to do and perhaps because those big brown eyes are hard to resist when the rest of the family is chowing down on the evening meal.

Feeding measured amounts twice a day also lets you keep tabs on what's normal for your dog in terms of appetite. A change of behavior may be an early clue that your dog is sick, since eating patterns, once set, are some of the most predictable of behaviors in a dog's life.

And don't just feed your pet the food that's on sale, what caught your eye at the grocery store or what your neighbor recommended. Nutrition is so important to the health and longevity of pets that we strongly urge you to ask your veterinarian for a specific recommendation on what food you should be feeding your pet.

Q: How can I tell if my dog is overweight?

A: When you think about the vast range of sizes and shapes dogs come in, you soon realize it would be impossible to make a single canine height-weight chart, such as those we're familiar with for people. How could you possibly compare dogs who are supposed to be stocky, like the Bulldog, with dogs who are supposed to be lean, like the Greyhound? And what's normal for a Pug is not going to work for a Cocker Spaniel.

That doesn't mean it's impossible to figure out if your dog's at her own proper weight for her size and body type. Proper weight for dogs is determined using a method called Body Conditioning Scoring (BCS).

Under the BCS system, a dog is at her normal weight if you can easily feel her ribs but they still have a slight cover of fat. The base of the tail, likewise, should have a slight fat cover, but not so much as to put a bump there or take away the correct smooth contour between the back and the tail. A dog of healthy weight will also have a tuck-in behind the rib cage, making for a well-defined waist.

At the high end of the BCS scale, an obese dog has ribs and a tail base that are difficult to feel under all the fat. From the top, her back could be used as a coffee table, and from the side view, fat is hanging down under her belly.

Most people would recognize a dog like that as fat, but you'd be surprised. Veterinarians see dogs waddle in with so much fat they can hardly breathe, and their owners will admit only to a "little" extra weight, having just been feeding the hairy blimp the proverbial "little handful" of food.

Even a little fat isn't good on a dog, by the way. So listen to your veterinarian and get your dog on a diet.

The obesity epidemic in dogs parallels the one in people. People, pets and the problem seem to be growing every day. What could be better than both you and your dog getting slim, fit and healthy together? There's a fitness plan that covers you both. The co-author of this book teamed with a top human physician to write Fitness Unleashed: A Dog and Owner's Guide to Losing Weight and Gaining Health Together. Drs. Marty Becker and Robert Kushner combined their expertise to come up with a way for a human and a dog to work together toward a healthier, thinner life—and probably a longer one, too.

Q: Why do dogs need vaccinations their whole lives, when people only get them as children?

A: **While vaccinations have saved** the lives of countless dogs, they're not without risk. That's one reason why guidelines for vaccinating pets have been changing in recent years.

The old idea that pets need "combination shots" (usually a combination of vaccines against distemper, adenovirus-2, leptospirosis, parainfluenza, parvovirus and corona virus) every year for protection against disease is being replaced with guidelines that tailor vaccines and schedules to an individual animal's needs.

This customized approach begins after the initial series of puppy vaccinations. Most boosters are then given at three-year intervals—some as needed and some not at all. It depends on where a dog lives and what kinds of risks he is exposed to. Rabies vaccinations, of course, are regulated by law because of the threat to human health. Most jurisdictions require those at three-year intervals, but in some places rabies shots are an annual event by law.

Only your veterinarian knows your pet's medical history, current health status, lifestyle and any emerging risks in the community. Talk with your vet about what combination of vaccines is necessary for your dog, and don't skip your pet's annual examination, even if he doesn't need shots every year.

Q: Can humans get diseases from their dogs?

A: If you think about all the diseases we could possibly contract from dogs—from rabies to worms, and more—it's almost enough to make you want to go pet free and wrap yourself up in plastic.

Scientists call these zoonotic diseases, and the U.S. Centers for Disease Control helpfully supplies a pretty scary list of them, even though the transmission of serious diseases from dogs to humans is rare.

Topping the list of potential concerns is rabies, a deadly disease more common in wildlife than in pets, thanks to decades of aggressive vaccination laws for dogs and other domesticated animals. Other concerns are bacterial—dogs are capable of transmitting salmonella, leptospirosis and campylobacteriosis, to name a nasty trio.

Diseases caused by parasites that we can get from our dogs include tapeworm, hookworm, roundworm, Lyme disease and giardia. And there's even ringworm, which is really a fungus.

Most times these diseases can be avoided by keeping your pet healthy (properly vaccinated and parasite free) and by practicing proper sanitary routines in your home—especially frequent hand-washing.

NEVER MIND DOCTOR'S ORDERS

A few years ago, I did a serious, scientifically based and very informative segment on ABC-TV's *Good Morning, America* on zoonoses—diseases that are transmissible between animals and people: nasty things ranging from rabies and ringworm, psittacosis and parasites, to giardia and cat scratch fever.

Staring straight into the camera, I told more than four million viewers that for reasons of science, sanitation and safety, they shouldn't let their pets lick them on the mouth and they shouldn't kiss their pets on the mouth.

That very same day, after a grueling commute from New York City back to my mountain oasis in Northern Idaho, I was greeted by the official welcoming committee of Almost Heaven Ranch: Scooter, the Wirehaired Fox Terrier, and Sirloin, the Labrador Retriever.

As they rushed to greet me in a delighted frenzy of fur—and we collided—I experienced a momentary surge of amnesia or was suffering from the dreaded childhood affliction of "liar, liar pants on fire." Because I proceeded to let both Scooter and Sirloin lick my face and give me the equivalent of a canine tonsil swab with their high-speed tongues.

How could I, as America's self-proclaimed "best-loved family doctor for pets," do the exact opposite of what I'd just prescribed for millions? Simply put, emotion got in the way of logic. My brain controlled the TV appearance, but my heart was in charge of the hero's welcome home courtesy of the family pets. And everyone knows that when your heart and your brain battle it out, the heart always wins.

—Dr. Marty Becker

Q: If a dog licks a wound, will it heal more quickly?

A: Honestly? Soap and water and a dab of antibiotic ointment is a much better option.

The main reason dogs lick their wounds is that the weepy moisture in the sore contains the sweet taste of blood sugar (glucose). The most valuable healing function of licking is that the dog's raspy tongue serves to debride (remove dead tissue) and clean (remove dirt, hair and other contaminants) the wound. Licking may also stimulate circulation, which hastens healing. Some scientists have claimed to have isolated chemicals in dog saliva that speed wound healing, but this appears to be a minor effect.

Q: I saw on TV that some dogs get braces. What's up with the Rin Tin grins?

A: Getting braces isn't just for humans anymore. Count the family pooch in, too. Rin Tin grins are typically done not because pets are vain, but because they are in pain. How would you like to have your teeth press into your gums or roof of your mouth every time you bit down or chewed? In fact, it's unethical for a veterinarian to perform any procedure on a dog for strictly cosmetic reasons.

Besides chewing, a dog uses her teeth much the way we use our hands—to explore and manipulate objects in her world. For a dog whose teeth don't meet or close properly, it's like a human trying to live without arms. There are health issues, too: Chewing can be painful for these dogs, who can become malnourished from not eating as much as they should.

Instead of moving multiple teeth, veterinary dentists move individual teeth in dogs, and the whole process can take as little as two to three months (as opposed to two to three years in humans). Dogs' teeth tend to stay in place, or are kept in place by the teeth surrounding them, so they don't need to wear retainers.

Rottweilers, Maltese and Poodles are particularly predisposed to orthodontic problems that can be fixed by wearing braces or otherwise moving teeth into a functional location. In other words, with the help of a skilled veterinary dentist, their bite can be just as good as their bark.

Q: With all this fancy canine dentistry, do dogs get root canals?

A: Dogs do get root canals and crowns, but they are fortunate enough to be completely anesthetized—out cold. So if everything is done properly, they won't hear the whir of the dental drill, smell the enamel being ground away, feel any pain or even know what happened.

When a dog's tooth breaks the nerve is exposed, which hurts just as much in pets as it does in people. Common causes include chewing on cow hooves, hard plastic toys and even rocks. Some veterinary dentists advise, "If you wouldn't want a dog's toy to hit you in the knee, it's too hard for your dog to be chewing on."

The most commonly fractured teeth are the canines (the long ones in the front, also called fangs or eye teeth) and the upper back premolars used for chewing. If untreated, infection will cause an abscess in the jawbone and spread throughout the system.

Because a dog's teeth are used for chewing, picking up and carrying objects, and to hold the lolling temperature regulator known as the tongue in place, fractured teeth often need a root canal and a crown. The alternative is removing the tooth entirely.

Leaving a fractured tooth with an exposed nerve is not an option. In most cases, root-canal therapy removes the internal infection and lets the dog retain her tooth forever. As with people, after the root canal a crown is placed on top of the tooth for support.

Q: Is a dog's mouth really cleaner than a human's?

A: *We're sorry, but . . . yuk!* You don't have to be an oral hygiene expert to know that any animal who eats cat poop, horse doo and garbage, who licks his own genitalia and is fascinated by the rear ends of other dogs, isn't exactly going to have a clean mouth. It's hard to imagine how such an idea ever got started, especially when you consider that we humans routinely floss and brush our teeth, gargle, visit the dentist and worry about the germs that cause bad breath.

So is a dog's mouth cleaner than a human's? Not at all!

Should you let your dog plant a big slurpy kiss on your cheek? Any public health expert will tell you no, but really . . . you'll likely be fine.

It's funny to realize, though, that even when you consider most humans take pride in having kissable breath and most hounds could care less about doggie breath, most people would much rather have a random dog kiss them than be French-kissed by any person they know.

PUPPY LOVE IN ANY LANGUAGE

A few years ago, a friend gave me a T-shirt that had on it an expression in French: *J'embrasse mon chien sur la bouche.* In English it means, "I kiss my dog on the lips," but the design didn't help anyone guess that. The shirt had nothing but words on it, no illustration.

As a result, total strangers would come up and ask me to explain what my shirt said. And over the handful of years before I wore it out, I noticed a big difference in the reactions to the translation.

The dog lovers would smile, sometimes laugh, and more than a few times would sheepishly admit they did the same thing.

But then there were those people whose smiling faces went very sour at the thought of kissing a dog at all, much less anywhere near the lips. The polite ones would recover with a wan smile and shrink away, as if I were somehow contaminated and possibly contagious. And then there were angry people who felt compelled to share their disgust of dogs, usually launching into a diatribe about a neighbor whose dog left calling cards on the lawn or barked all night.

And then they'd stand there, waiting for me to defend all dogs and all dog owners because . . . well, I kiss my dogs on the lips. Vive la différence!

—Gina Spadafori

Q: Is there a cure for doggie breath?

A: **Doggie breath is a euphemism** for any odor that's a kissing cousin to putrid. Veterinarians will tell you that sometimes a dog's breath enters the examination room while the dog is still in the waiting area.

Doggie breath should come as no surprise. Humans know we don't have kissable breath if we skip brushing our pearly whites for just one day, and dogs never floss, brush or gargle. Not to mention all the things some dogs eat—and we really don't want to mention that stuff again!

But while your dog will eventually exhale the last smell of the "snacks" she consumed from the cat's litter box, some bad breath never goes away. That's because most dogs don't just have bad breath—their mouth is sick.

Oral disease is the number one health problem in dogs, with as many as 80 percent of dogs showing signs of oral disease by the age of three. What starts out as plaque and tartar buildup may progress to diseases such as periodontal disease (where the gums and bony support structures for teeth are eaten away) and systemic problems with vital organs such as the liver, kidneys and heart.

The risk and severity of oral disease varies. Small breeds are more prone to dental disease because their teeth are crowded together and don't get as clean just from chewing toys and dry food; the bone around their teeth is also thinner and thus is destroyed faster. Smaller dogs also live longer, giving the mechanisms of dental disease longer to do their damage. Dogs who have compromised health or are malnourished can't fight the bacteria that lead to periodontal disease.

Some pet food companies have developed foods to help keep teeth and gums healthy (vets call them edible toothbrushes), but the biggest advantage you can give your dog in the fight against dental disease is to pick up a toothbrush. Use toothbrushes and toothpastes designed for dogs (who can't swish and spit, after all), along with veterinary dental wipes and protective gels.

Chewing will help to keep teeth clean, as well, and there are plenty of products designed to provide safe, healthy and satisfying gnawing for your dog.

Studies have shown that dogs with good oral health live 15 percent longer or an average of about two years! Make regular dental examinations and cleaning part of your dog's preventive health regimen. Your veterinarian will be able to help you choose appropriate products to keep you pal's breath sweet.

Q: Do some dogs get plastic surgery? What about Bowser Botox?

A: **Sometimes a dog's facial folds** or lower eyelid will roll inward, and eyelashes or hair will rub across the surface of the cornea. You know how a single eyelash can seem like torture to your eyeball? Imagine the erosive action of a veritable hairbrush on the eye of a breed at risk for facial fold defects, such as the Bulldog, Pekingese, Shar-Pei or Pug. The condition can cause extreme discomfort, and vision loss is a possibility.

While surgery is the more common—and permanent—way of dealing with this problem, Botox has reportedly been used to get the inverted eyelid or wayward facial fold to return to its normal position.

Yes, both treatments change the dog's looks. But really, it's all about comfort, not vanity.

Q: Is it true that dogs have cat fleas?

A: Yes, but don't blame the cats.

In 1834, a Frenchman by the name of Bouché took a flea off a cat, described it in the scientific literature and gave it the name *Pulex felis* (*felis* is Latin for cat). He actually got the first part, the genus, wrong, but he was the first to use *felis* as a species name for a flea. The Entomological Society gives all insects common names, so *Ctenocephalides felis* (with the correct genus) was officially named the cat flea.

Bouché could have taken the same flea species from a dog, fox or lynx in France, and today we might be calling it the dog, fox or lynx flea. There is a dog flea (*Ctenocephalides canis*), which, as you might suspect, was first described after its removal from a dog. However, this is a rare species and has seldom been caught in a flea comb in North America over the past twenty years. In most countries, the cat flea is the most common flea found on both dogs and cats.

There are about 500 different kinds of fleas, each named for their meal of preference. There's even a human flea!

Q: Do dogs get Alzheimer's disease?

A: **Dogs are living longer** and are prone to many of the same age-related health problems as their human companions. One of the most devastating is Canine Cognitive Dysfunction, which is very similar to human Alzheimer's. This condition affects millions of dogs and leads to reduced brain function and, often, behavioral changes.

Like the human Alzheimer's patient, the dog often seems to forget her surroundings and not recognize loved ones. Or she may act confused or disoriented, may sleep more during the day and less at night or even have frequent housetraining lapses.

Imagine going from a world of color and surround sound to black-and-white images with the sound coming from an AM radio. That's what it's like for your beloved senior dog with Canine Cognitive Dysfunction.

In some cases, a change of diet may help. Others need the addition of a drug specifically developed to treat Canine Cognitive Dysfunction, which can help your pal feel more like herself again. Check with your veterinarian about the diet and medications.

Q: My veterinarian gave me a prescription that had to be filled at a human pharmacy. Later, I read about Prozac for pets. Are human drugs safe for pets?

A: Many pet lovers are amused when they hear about human drugs such as Prozac being prescribed for pets, but in fact, it's nothing new. If they couldn't use drugs marketed and approved for use in human medicine, veterinarians would not be able to provide the best care for pets.

Veterinarians are allowed to use these drugs because they've been accepted as part of standard practice, based on widespread documentation in research literature, textbooks and other professional forums.

There may be differences, however, in why the medication is being used. Lasix (furosemide) is used in both humans and animals to control the fluid buildup caused by heart problems. Prozac isn't used to treat depression in dogs as it is in humans, but is often part of a regimen of medication and behavior/environmental modification intended to correct such problems as separation anxiety.

Your veterinarian should explain the risks and benefits of each drug prescribed for your pet. Ask as many questions as you need to, until you are clear about exactly what the medicine is for and how, when, and for how long you must give it to your dog. Contact the clinic immediately if you have any concerns.

It's critically important for pet lovers to realize that not all human medicines can be given to pets. If you're thinking of giving your pet any drug—even an herbal remedy or over-the-counter product—check with your veterinarian first. What's good for you may be harmful for your dog.

Q: I read that some dogs take Viagra, even neutered ones. Why?

A: It's true that neutered male dogs have no need for help in the sex department. After neutering, they have no interest, either.

Viagra, though, is sometimes prescribed for both pets and people to help ease the symptoms of severe pulmonary hypertension—high pressure in the vessels of the lungs. This disease is physically debilitating and many affected dogs are unable to walk across the room without collapsing. Once they receive the proper dose of Viagra, these dogs can take short, daily walks with their owners and return to a more normal life.

Q: Do dogs sweat?

A: Compared to their owners, dogs have very few sweat glands. There are some in the paw pads, so dogs do sweat from their feet and from other relatively less furry regions of their bodies. But the primary way dogs cool off is by panting.

Panting is very rapid, shallow breathing that enhances the evaporation of water from the tongue, mouth and upper respiratory tract. Evaporation dissipates heat as water vapor.

Dogs will also lick themselves, spreading saliva over their body and limbs, which provides minor amounts of heat loss by evaporation. (Don't believe it? Try licking yourself on a hot day and see what happens.) Lying on their backs facilitates heat loss through the less hairy parts on the canine belly.

Despite an effective heat-exchange mechanism in panting, dogs can still rapidly overheat. Common signs of overheating include intense thirst, weakness, discomfort and anxiety. An overheated dog seeks shade and cold floors, and may rest in a frog-leg position. Heat stroke is serious, can develop within minutes, and can be fatal without immediate veterinary intervention. (And sometimes even with.)

Prevention is better than treatment: Keep pets quiet, cool and calm on hot days and provide lots of cool water—and leave the athletics for the cooler weather.

Panting can reach frequencies of 300 to 400 breaths per minute (the normal canine breathing rate is 30 to 40 breaths per minute). Yet it requires surprisingly little effort. Because of the natural elasticity of the lungs and airways, panting does not expend much energy nor create additional heat.

Q: How can dogs walk on hot or cold surfaces without hurting their feet?

A: **The thickness of a dog's paw pads** helps them go "barefoot" on various types of terrain. Dogs also have two more legs to distribute the weight, which is an advantage on rough ground.

That doesn't mean a dog can't use a little extra protection. Sled dogs often wear booties, although on ice they get better traction without them, using their nails like cleats. City dogs wear booties in the winter, too, when they can protect a dog's feet from salt and other chemicals on sidewalks.

Q: When a dog drags his bottom along the ground, does that mean he has worms?

A: Not necessarily. Dogs scoot to amuse the family or embarrass you in front of houseguests. Just kidding! A dog scoots across the carpet or grass on his rear to relieve an itch or irritation. Parasites such as tapeworms and roundworms can be pretty irritating, but so, too, can impacted or infected anal sacs, or fecal material that is clinging to the hair around the anus.

While some dog owners give their pet what is sometimes called a "potty path trim," cutting the hair around a dog's anus is a delicate business. You can also check on your dog's anal glands yourself, but think about whether you really want to. "Expressing" the anal glands regularly (squeezing out the foul-smelling contents—hopefully, into a clean paper towel) isn't difficult to learn, but the technique and smell are definitely not for the squeamish.

This is why dealing with a dog's behind is often left to professionals, either veterinarians or groomers. If your dog is scooting, let one of them take a look.

If you think you see evidence of parasites around the rectum or in the dog's stool—tapeworm segments, for example, look like grains of uncooked rice—take a fresh sample of the feces to the veterinarian right away for an accurate diagnosis.

Q: Can dogs get sunburned?

A: **The risks of overexposure to the sun** can, indeed, be a problem for many dogs. Not only can they get sunburned, they can also get skin cancer.

Dogs most at risk for skin disease and cancer caused by the sun are those with short, white coats, light-colored skin and sparse tummy fur. Breeds with these characteristics include Dalmatians, Bull Terriers, Staffordshire Bull Terriers, Whippets, Italian Greyhounds and Greyhounds. The more sun exposure, the greater the risk.

Skin cancer can strike dogs as young as four years old, which is why prevention is extremely important. Decreasing exposure is the only way to protect an animal from sun-related problems. Don't let your dog sunbathe, put a roof or awning over outdoor runs and consider dressing your smart pooch in a solar protective T-shirt.

What about sunblock? Absolutely! Use a children's waterproof product with no scent on hairless areas, such as the tips of the ears and the top of the nose.

Q: Is it really true that when a dog's nose is cold and wet, it means she's healthy?

A:

Sort of. To really get to the bottom of this, we need to understand why a dog's nose is wet in the first place. Tears are constantly produced to lubricate the movement of the eyes. Because this lubrication is so critical to eye health, the dog's body routine produces more tears than are needed. These excess tears flow through the naso-lacrimal (literally "nose-tears") duct and out the base of the nose. (People experience this when crying.)

As the tears drip down into the dog's face, the dog licks her nose, spreading the tear fluid over the nose, which wets it. Then, evaporation causes the nose to be cool. The moistened nose is better equipped to dissolve airborne chemicals, which contributes to a better sense of smell.

When a dog is sick, the body uses up more internal water in the process of fighting disease. This increased use, especially with a fever, causes relative dehydration, even if the dog is drinking a normal amount of water.

This dehydration results in decreased tear production, and hence a dry nose.

However, the same dry nose could be because of fluid loss from panting on a hot day. Some dogs (such as Poodles and Lhasa Apsos) often get reddened cheeks from blocked tear ducts, so there is less fluid flowing through the ducts to moisten the nose. The bottom line is that the dry nose is one indicator of hydration, but it indicates illness only if it's coupled with lethargy and other symptoms.

A calm, relaxed dog officially has a fever when you either stick a thermometer where the sun doesn't shine or use one of the new instant ear thermometers and determine the dog's temperature is above 102.5 degrees Fahrenheit.

Q: Does that "seven human years equal one dog year" formula really work?

A: **Not really.** Still, you can see how this idea got started. Something in the neighborhood of seventy is a decent life span for a human being, while ten years is probably average for a lot of dogs—although some, especially small ones, live far longer. Divide 70 by 10 and what do you get? Seven.

But if you look at a one-year-old dog, you can see that he's an adult—sexually mature and very close to being physically and mentally mature. A dog's development at this age is far beyond that of a seven-year-old human child. In short, the seven-equals-one rule just doesn't fit a dog's early years.

The first eight months of a dog's life equals about thirteen years in human terms: birth to puberty, in other words. At one year old, a dog is the equivalent of an eighteen-year-old human with a little filling out still to do. After the age of two, when a dog is about twenty-one in human terms, every dog year equals approximately five human ones.

These are ballpark estimates, of course, because the fact is, dogs age at very different rates. Small dogs may hit puberty at five months, while some larger dogs may be more than a year and a half old before a female comes into heat for the first time.

So when is a dog "old"? Giant breeds such as Great Danes are senior citizens at six; a Labrador Retriever may be considered old at eight. A little dog like the Pomeranian could behave like a healthy adult well into the double digits.

Q: If dogs are carnivores, why isn't dog food nothing but meat?

A: Feeding a dog didn't used to be something you stayed up nights worrying about. They ate what we gave them. They ate what we left behind. They ate what other animals left behind. They killed things to eat, and they ate the remains of what other animals killed. In other words, they got along as best they could with whatever we gave them and whatever they scrounged up.

Unlike cats, who are true carnivores and have very little use for nonmeat food items, dogs are carnivores with some wiggle room. They can survive on all kinds of foods, and do—as do many animals who aren't above scavenging.

The this-and-that approach to dog feeding worked well enough for generations, especially when most dogs lived in rural areas and could supplement their diets with the occasional rodent in the barn, rabbit in the field, leftovers in the farmer's kitchen and offal from the butchering of livestock. But as more dogs became urban and suburban dwellers—and leash laws came into play, making hunting less and less likely—living off the land became pretty tough for a dog.

From great social change always comes great business opportunity . . . in this case, the pet-food industry was born. Commercial pet foods really took off after World War II, when America was starting to put a premium on convenience and our ability to produce food grew and grew.

Many pet foods started off as a way to use leftovers from food produced for people, but that's not really the case today. As pets have gained status in our families, pet-food companies have responded. Today you can find hundreds of product lines at every price level and with all kinds of ingredients, all based on decades of research into what keeps a dog healthy.

And surprise! It's not just meat. Grains have become a mainstay in pet food because they are a good protein source at a reasonable price, and because foods that combine meat, grains and other ingredients are stable enough to be shipped, stored and stay fresh until you can dish them out.

Generations of dogs have lived long and healthy lives on commercial pet foods that combine multiple sources of protein, not just those made primarily from meat.

Not that dogs ever survived on meat alone, anyway.

What we think of as "meat," flesh and muscle, is only a part of the natural diet of a wild canine. In fact, wild canines also eat skin, bones, guts and even stomach contents of their prey. A pampered pet dining on nothing but filet mignon is not being well served—and would eventually become ill from malnutrition.

Q: Is it ever safe to give poultry bones to my dog?

A: **There's no argument** that cooked poultry bones should be off the menu for all dogs, all the time. On this point, everyone agrees. The bones easily splinter (we humans can crack them with our own teeth) and form sharp little shards that can stick in any part of the dog's digestive tract, from one end to the other.

Raw poultry bones, however, are fed by many dog owners as part of a diet that is quite controversial. Here's the lowdown.

In recent years, a very small but growing number of dog lovers have started preparing their dog's meals at home, using raw, fresh and often organic ingredients: meat and bones, primarily, but also ground-up vegetables and, in some cases, grains.

Some of these feeding regimens are lumped under the acronym BARF, which stands for "biologically appropriate raw food" (or sometimes, "bones and raw flesh"). The idea behind these diets is that dogs are carnivores, so they should eat in a way that approximates as closely as possible the diet their wild relatives feed themselves. Raw poultry pieces are popular in many of these diets, bones and all.

And yet, an overwhelming majority of veterinarians have opinions on raw diets—and especially those with raw bones—that range from skeptical to downright negative, for reasons that include bacterial contamination from handling raw meat (say hello to my friend salmonella!), incomplete nutrition and digestive problems resulting from wolfing down raw poultry bones. Many of these problems can be avoided by making adjustments in how the diet is prepared and fed, but the research, time and money involved in preparing a proper homemade diet is realistically beyond what most dog lovers are willing to do.

To sum it all up: Cooked poultry bones? Everyone agrees: No! No! Raw poultry bones? Hey, they're controversial even among those people who feed a home-prepared raw diet, many of whom purchase and use industrial-strength meat grinders rather than give their dogs whole bones.

Q: It's obvious dogs have a better sense of smell than humans do. How much better?

A: **Humans have about five million** scent receptors in their noses; dogs have about two hundred million. Dogs can detect tiny levels of odors, even if they make up just a few parts per billion in the air or in a liquid. Their noses are also uniquely designed to draw in air samples for analysis.

Of course, not all canine noses are created equal. You're not going to see a dog with a pushed-in muzzle, like a Boston Terrier, tracking someone on *America's Most Wanted.* That's because in breeding for a short face—a face more like ours—we've reduced the real estate available for scent receptors in some breeds.

On the other end of the scale, a breed developed for tracking, such as the Bloodhound, has a sense of smell so keen that the results of his work are admissible in a court of law. In addition to a long, deep muzzle, the Bloodhound has ears to sweep scent up from the ground and skin folds to hold scents around his face.

Dogs have been used to detect drugs and explosives for generations, of course, and to find people who are on the lam or just lost. But in recent years dogs have been trained for some truly innovative scent detection work, including sniffing out cancerous tissue, smuggled food, counterfeit DVDs, termites, bedbugs and more.

Q: Is it true dogs can't see in color?

A: **Dogs do see colors,** but not as many as we can see. And the colors they see aren't as rich, either. This may be a relief to some of us, who are tired of hearing how dogs smell better, hear better, and are faster and stronger than we are.

The bottom line, though, is that dogs don't have great color vision because they don't need it. If you throw a tennis ball in the grass, the yellow color makes it easier for you to find, not your dog, who could find a blue tennis ball much more easily. Your dog doesn't care; she's going to find it with her nose.

Dog vision is exactly what you'd expect from an animal whose life depends on her ability to spot prey. We humans developed with the ability to see in rich color and detail, while a dog's vision is more closely attuned to catching movement. The better to eat you with, my dear!

Q: Why do dogs circle, scratch and paw the floor before they lie down?

A: Every year your authors go to a massive pet industry trade show called Global Pet Expo, where pet product manufacturers show off their goods to thousands of retail buyers. And every year it seems the number and variety of dog beds has increased by at least half. Round beds, square beds, fluffy beds, firm beds, covered beds, hammock beds—it's difficult to imagine a concept in dog beds that hasn't yet shown up in pet supply stores.

Of course, things weren't always as cushy.

Before the days of damask-covered, scented cedar beds with removable, washable inner liners gently nestled in frames of kiln-dried, stained and varnished oak with the dog's name etched across the front panel, dogs had . . . dirt, leaves and maybe a few small branches. And hey, for a farm dog, there was always . . . hay. Pawing it into the shape of a nest made everything more comfortable, the bowl shape helped retain the dog's body heat and you could see better to boot (for Spot to spot potential friend, foe or dinner). Scratching the ground also puts a dog's scent there, a nonliquid way to say, "This spot is mine." (Because even dogs do not like to wet the bed.)

These days, with so many comfortable beds, the circle, paw and scratch routine probably isn't really that necessary. But still, a dog likes to get his sleeping spot "just right"—whether there's an actual bed there or not. After all, we bet you have your own bedtime rituals, fluffing your pillows, folding your comforter . . . and pushing the dog off your side of the bed.

FOR DOGS, THE "GOOD OLD DAYS" ARE NOW

The e-mail was one of those funny ones that arrive unexpected; the joke that you and millions of other people all get at roughly the same time—usually in multiple copies.

This one, labeled "for baby boomers," made light of how safety-oriented we are today, how our kids are practically bubble-wrapped with protective gear when they play, as opposed to the boomer kids about whom no one worried as long as they were home before dark. I smiled, remembering the days before children had schedules more complicated than a doctor's and parents had worries more pressing than the president's.

Until I got to the final line of this celebration of "the good old days": "Our dogs ran loose and never went to the vet."

Sorry, but the nostalgia stops there. I remember those days, too, with a lot less fondness. I remember roaming family dogs who died of distemper, being hit by cars, or getting lost. I remember fleas running rampant, and the way dogs smelled from untreated skin conditions and rotting teeth. I remember how training a pet used to mean punishing the animal instead of teaching and rewarding good behavior.

Sorry, but I like leash laws for dogs. I prefer to see animals trained cooperatively, rather than through force and fear. And I much appreciated having a dog who recently lived to be almost sixteen, happy and healthy until the day before he died—and for that I thank our veterinarians and all the improvements in care that have become common in the last couple of decades.

The good old days? For our pets, they're now.

—Gina Spadafori

Q: Why do dogs need to have their nails trimmed? Won't walking around wear them down naturally?

A: If your dog put in as many miles a day as her wild cousins, through sand or over rocky outcroppings, you could probably put those nail trimmers away. But most of today's dogs are treading on carpet or grass, and the amount of time a modern dog spends on the move—even on concrete—simply isn't enough to have much of an impact on the length of her nails. Which means you're going to have to keep up with those pup-icures.

The groomer will be happy to cut them for you, and so will the technicians at your veterinarian's office. The problem is, by the time you get around to asking for help, your dog's nails are pretty long, making a bad situation even worse for all concerned. The more bad experiences your dog has getting her nails trimmed, the harder she'll fight you the next time. Some dogs become so resistant that they'll resort to biting—and you'll have to resort to a soft muzzle to get done what should be a routine, pain-free grooming task.

Yes, there is a better way! Start right from the beginning, and teach your dog slowly and with lots of treats to tolerate trimming.

If you're using nail clippers, take the tool in hand and touch it to your dog's feet, then her toes, then the nails, while praising her and giving her treats for each step. When she is used to having her feet handled, put the clipper against the nail and praise and treat more still. Don't cut anything yet. Just get her used to the idea of you touching her feet with a tool in your hand.

When all is calm, trim off just a little, and so on, working up to a full pedicure. Praise and more praise! Treats and more treats! Don't insist on getting all the nails done at once. Do one or two toes a night, and put the clippers away while both you and the dog are feeling positive about the experience.

Some dogs prefer having their nails filed instead of clipped, perhaps because with a grinder it's easy to stop before you hit the quick. (The quick is that little bundle of nerves and blood vessels that runs down the center of the nail.) You can buy a canine nail grinder, or just use a lightweight rotary grinding tool, such as the Dremmel.

Again, you'll be working up to the end result very slowly, giving treats at first for seeing the grinder, seeing the grinder near the feet, listening to the grinder, listening to the grinder near the feet. Treats! Praise! Patience!

Yes, we know you wish walks on concrete would do the job, but they won't, so you're going to have to deal with it. Slowly. And with rewards. Hey, give yourself a few treats as well. You deserve them.

Q: How much time do dogs normally spend sleeping?

A: A dog can spend more than half his life asleep—ten to thirteen hours a day, and older dogs spend even more time sleeping. Some breeds are more active than others (think Jack Russell Terrier vs. Basset Hound), and outdoor dogs spend more time awake than indoor dogs.

The weather can also change a dog's sleep; pets will tend to sleep more on cloudy days than sunny ones, and snuggle up more on cold days than warm ones.

A visit to your veterinarian is in order if your dog seems to be sleeping significantly more than usual and is lethargic, or sleeps significantly less and is hyperactive or aggressive when awake.

While it probably won't come as a surprise to readers of this book, studies reveal that seven of ten Americans who share their homes with pets also share their beds. Nighty-night!

Q: Is it true that only domesticated dogs sleep on their backs?

A: Many people believe that dogs are the only members of the canine family who sleep on their backs. In fact, wild coyotes, foxes and even captive wolves will also sleep belly up.

Two conditions need to be met for this behavior: The animal has to feel safe in his surroundings, and he has to be warm. On cold days, even a happy dog will sleep curled up to conserve body heat.

Q: Why do dogs bury bones, and how do they remember where they put them?

A: *Yummy, yummy bones!* The dirtier, stinkier and slimier the better! Such is the opinion of many dogs who, after having gnawed off the choicest bits of meat, decide it's time to put the bone in a safe place to "age," like a fine wine. Because a dog is nothing if not a gourmand of the highest standards, wouldn't you agree?

No? Well, you're right. In fact, dogs bury bones (that is to say, some dogs bury bones, because not all do) because in the old days, before refrigerators, before neat bags of kibble, before custom lids for saving canned dog food . . . heck, before two-legged buddies to dish it all out, wild dogs and wolves were on their own. Sometimes they got lucky and there was elk for all. Sometimes they went hungry, unless they put a little aside for an unlucky day.

Which is why, even today, when our dogs have little doubt where their next meal is coming from, something deep and primeval tells them that it might be a good idea to bank that bone in the dirt. And once the bone is buried, how about saving a little something extra, just in case. The TV remote, perhaps? The filched flip-flop? And . . . well, you never know when you're going to need a tennis ball, do you?

But back to the bones. Burying makes sense, or rather, it used to, and back then it was a pretty decent survival strategy. A bone in the dirt is protected from flies and maggots. The scraps are out of the sun and in a dirt-icebox of sorts, especially in colder climates. Buried, a bone may escape the notice of other hungry creatures; then again, it may not. But if you put enough bits and pieces underground, you may just have enough to survive.

That is, if you remember where you buried everything.

Do they? It's more likely dogs locate their buried treasure with their incredible noses, because memory isn't really their strong suit.

When it comes to digging, some breeds are much more into it than others. Terriers probably top the list, and no surprise there—the word "terrier" comes from the Latin terra, which means "earth." These dogs are literally named for their interest in digging, not only to find vermin in their underground burrows or to bury bones, but also just for the sheer joy of it.

Some northern breeds are prodigious diggers, too—
into the snow if they're trying to duck the wind chill,
and into the cool earth if they're escaping the heat.
If you had a plush double coat that you could never take off,
you'd probably do a little summer digging, too.

Q: Why do dogs always sniff each other when they meet?

A: *The mouth, genitals and anus* are areas with the highest concentrations of smell. That's true in people, as well, but those are smells we usually prefer to avoid. Dogs, however, can read smell like an encyclopedia—and the places where the smell is strongest are always the bestsellers. It's only natural for animals as smell-oriented as dogs, who think of sniffing urine, feces and saliva as the human equivalent of Google.

When two dogs meet, generally it will be the more dominant dog who initiates "private" sniffing (actually, to dogs no part of the anatomy is private) under the tail, so one function of the sniffing dance is to establish hierarchy.

Sniffing under the tail also establishes identity. The anal glands produce a powerfully pungent odor. (Taken to an extreme, these are the same glands that are used as weapons by skunks.) The smell from these glands is as one-of-a-kind to a dog as a fingerprint is to us.

The dogs are also checking out the smell of urine. We humans can't even begin to imagine the information a dog can get from a single drop, including gender, age, if a female dog is in season, whether a dog has been exercising, if he is stressed and more.

Simply put, the nose knows. A couple of sniffs and a dog understands everything about another dog, which is why dogs dive for the information at the source.

Q: When dogs lick each other's mouths, are they kissing?

A: Licking a more dominant animal's lips started out, behaviorally speaking, as an attempt to get food: When wild dogs are transitioning from mother's milk to semisolid food, they mob their mom, licking her muzzle to prompt her to regurgitate semidigested food for her babies. (Yet another example of how dogs love to eat things we find disgusting.)

But this behavior becomes just as much about trying to get acceptance. You can see dogs doing it in any dog park. Younger, timid or less socially dominant animals will lower themselves and reach up to lick the lips of the dogs they see as their betters. It's not really a kiss, but more of a salute—a nonviolent way to establish or reestablish social order so every canine can get along without more physical (and possibly more dangerous) displays of rank.

In other words, among people a kiss may be just a kiss, but among dogs it's a whole lot more.

PUP-A-RAZZI

The woman sitting next to me on the airplane kept peeking over my shoulder, looking at the veterinary magazines I was reading. I was in full-press work mode, so I'd offered her little more than a gracious and cheerful hello when we first boarded.

Finally, after about an hour, she could take it no longer and asked, "Are you a veterinarian?" Knowing the rest of the flight would now be dedicated to her, I put everything away, looked her in the eye and said "yes."

"I knew it!" she said. The floodgates were now open. "I have a Cocker Spaniel named Joe (get it, Joe Cocker), who's my baby. My husband travels a lot and my kids are grown, so most of the time it's just the two of us, which is fine by me."

At this point I tried to get beyond eye contact and nodding my head in agreement by joining in the conversation. I opened my mouth to say something, but her verbal machine-gun fire was unrelenting. So I went back to just listening and nodding in agreement. Veterinarians get used to this.

Finally she brought out the ultimate weapon of proud mothers everywhere: photos.

These days, pet photos know no boundaries. They're included with Christmas letter photo montages, sit on our desks at work, adorn our refrigerators at home and electronically bounce from computer to computer. We've all seen photo key chains of people with their pets, photo buttons, wallet photos. But few people have had to spend two hours of a three-hour flight looking at a three-ring binder showcasing the happy life of Joe Cocker.

While fellow pet lovers are more than happy to delight someone by cooing and doing eyebrow flashes at every photo, pet photos are like Kryptonite to those who do not love animals. The proud pet mom goes from photo to photo saying, "Look at this photo. Doesn't Joe look cute lying there on my husband's pillow while he's off on his business trip?" But to people who choose to live their lives with nothing but humans in their bed, all those pet photos look exactly the same.

Which is why, as an ardent pet lover, I am willing to bear the cross of being a vet by looking at everybody's pet pictures. Still, I, too, have my limits.

The last time I visited my mother's house in Twin Falls, Idaho, I noticed many pictures of Becker Schnauzers, past and present. There were clusters of photos on the end table featuring beloved past pets Pepsi, Katie and Ginger. A recent photo of the latest hairy princess, Peanut Butter, was proudly displayed, framed in expensive sterling silver. There was even an original oil painting of the Schnauzers on the wall in a gilded frame.

Were the gold-encrusted paintings of the Schnauzers occasionally interspersed with pictures of my brothers and sisters and me? Our families? Her grandchildren? Nope. Just the dogs.

—Dr. Marty Becker

Q: Why do sirens and other wailing noises make dogs howl?

A: **Howling is fun.** It's like canine choral group singing, or picking up the microphone at a canine karaoke machine; a way for dogs scattered across a few miles and separated by fences to get in touch with their inner wolf and be part of something bigger—a pack!

It was once thought that sirens hurt the sensitive ears of dogs and the howling was a protest of pain. But now most behaviorists think it's an instinctive group behavior. The right noise—a siren, or even certain notes on a viola—will get a dog lifting his nose to the sky, and wooo-wooo-wooing. Other dogs just can't help but join in.

As with digging, some breeds are more prone to howling than others. The wolflike northern breeds seem to take to it naturally, as do hounds such as Beagles and Bassets, with their distinctive baying.

Q: Is there really such a thing as "pack mentality"? Do good dogs go bad in packs?

A: **Like people, dogs are social animals.** And like people, dogs can gain confidence in a group, then do things they would never do alone. Think of it as the canine "mob mentality."

So yes, both dogs and people can do bad things when they're in a bad group, feeding off the energy of those around them. If one dog starts barking, chasing or biting, the others may join in.

Q: Why do some dogs threaten each other when they're on the opposite sides of a fence but get along fine if the fence is removed?

A: Just as with people, some dogs are a lot tougher when they don't think they'll actually have to step up and fight. Some fence-fighters won't back down if the fence falls, but a lot of them will.

It also depends on what the fence is fencing in: A dog may feel the need to defend her home turf. Both the dog who's tough only behind the fence and the one who'd fight if the fence falls may be fine with other dogs if they meet away from their own territory.

Then there are those dogs who've just learned to enjoy fence-running. To them, it's all a game.

Q: What's the best way to stop a dogfight?

A: **Never let one start.** Become familiar with your dog's body language and behavior. A hard stare is usually the first indication of too much interest in another dog.

If you miss the early signs and a fight starts, you need to get the dogs separated as quickly and safely as possible. If there are two people around, each should grab the back legs of one of the combatants, pulling back and upward so that each dog is upended. Don't let them down on all fours until the fight is out of them—no more snarling, growling or lunging—and then take the dogs away from each other.

If you're alone when a fight breaks out, turn on a hose full blast and drench the dogs. A gallon of white vinegar will also do the trick, but once you get the dogs apart you'll have to rinse them off. The vinegar can sting if it gets in the eyes, but it will do far less damage than a dogfight will.

Never reach into a fight to try and grab the dogs' collars; you'll likely be bitten. And do not scream at the dogs, since they'll see you as the ringside cheering section, and your adrenaline will keep them going.

It's up to a dog's owner to prevent injuries—to dogs and to people—by being aware of their dog's behavior at all times. Don't wait for something to happen. Protect your dog from situations where he might become involved in a dogfight. If you're at a dog park and a dog comes in who seems scary . . . leave!

Q: Do dogs learn better with praise or punishment?

A: It's not so much an issue of how dogs learn—praise and punishment both work—but rather, what kind of relationship you'd like to have with your dog. Because reward-based training systems using food and praise seem to work very well without hurting or traumatizing a dog, most dog training these days is on the positive side.

Although people have always trained dogs, the boot-camp style of dog training that so many pet lovers learned came from—hey, big surprise here—former military dog trainers. In the last couple of decades, the emphasis on force and "breaking" a dog has shifted, and dog owners are encouraged to use treats and praise—along with management of a dog's environment to keep her out of trouble—to mold and reward correct behavior.

Part of the reason for this change is a better understanding of how we want our family dogs to learn, so that we end up with a stable, unaggressive animal who is safe around children.

So yes, you can punish a dog and she'll learn. Unfortunately, one of the things she'll learn is that you're not particularly nice or reasonable. Training that relies on reward-based lessons, when properly followed, will develop your dog's manners along with your relationship. Seems like a better deal to us!

THE DOG TRAINER'S MEETING

Some twenty years ago I went to my first meeting of the Dog Writers Association of America, which is held annually in New York City. The DWAA was formed more than seventy-five years ago by a small group of sportswriters who covered dog shows, back in the day when newspapers considered these events to be newsworthy beyond the annual fuss over the winner of the Westminster Kennel Club dog show.

Today, the DWAA's membership consists of people who work in all kinds of media—newspapers, magazines, books, Internet, radio and television. The only thing they have in common is an interest in dogs. Not surprisingly, quite a few members have many years of experience in training dogs.

That first meeting I attended had some controversy, but I was too new to the group to know (or care) much about the issues involved. So I took a seat in the back of the room and just listened. And I soon realized that the DWAA members used the same voice and body language dogs use with each other—and that good dog trainers use with their dogs.

When trying to argue their points, each of the DWAA members dropped the pitch of their voice and pulled themselves up on their toes like terriers who'd spotted a rat. They made clear, bold eye contact, and even averted their eyes submissively when conceding a point!

To this day, I don't remember the topics of discussion, but I clearly remember the body language of the people in the room. It was like watching wolves on a nature show—and I've seen the same show at almost every gathering of dog experts since.

—Gina Spadafori

Q: Why is it so hard to teach a dog to come when called?

A: First, let it be said that no command is more important for a dog to learn than "come" as it may very well save his life someday. Some dog owners don't take the time to train their pet to come when called—or if they do, they don't take the time to train the dog completely, so he understands the command in the face of increasingly more interesting distractions.

Other owners inadvertently train their dogs not to come by calling the dog to do something he doesn't like. This might be calling the dog to come to face a mess, a bath or even just leaving his buddies behind at the dog park. Soon enough, the dog learns that "come" means "come get something you definitely don't want." Would you come under those circumstances?

On top of that, people make things worse by getting angry if the dog is reluctant to come, making it even less likely a dog will come next time he is called.

Some breeds and breed mixes are more naturally inclined than others to want to return to you when called, but the fact is that no dog is untrainable. You just need to train them the right way. Get help from a trainer.

In the meantime, if you're faced with a loose dog, try "sit" instead. Many dogs know the command "sit" much better than they know "come." If your dog is on the lam and you can't get him to come to you by calling him—even if you crouch down and open your arms—you can sometimes get him by asking him to sit and then taking hold of his collar.

If that doesn't work, don't chase your dog. That's just a cool game that he absolutely must join in by running away from you. Instead, try running away from your dog, in the hope of triggering his chase reflex.

Knowing these tricks may save your dog's life. When they do, get help from a trainer so your dog comes when called and you don't have to trick him next time.

Q: Why do some dogs go crazy when they see people in uniform?

A: It's not just women who love people in uniform! So what is it about the mail carrier or others in uniform that makes even friendly dogs go off like a trigger-happy cowboy? The answer, according to dog trainers, is that they learn this aggressive routine. Here's how it works.

It's natural for a dog to bark in warning when a stranger comes to the door. In the case of the mail carrier, that stranger comes almost every day at about the same time. The dog barks to alert the family and to suggest (in language any dog can understand) that the stranger is about to invade protected territory—protected by the dog, that is.

And then the stranger leaves! From the dog's point of view, it was her brave warning that sent the interloper packing. She doesn't realize the mail carrier's just going on to the next house. As the dog sees it, she barked and the interloper left.

Over time, the dog's reaction intensifies as she tries harder to send a message to the stranger, who just doesn't seem to learn to keep away. As the dog becomes more and more worked up over time by this routine, the potential for a bite increases. Even friendly dogs become conditioned and want to nail the mail carrier. Eventually, this reaction becomes generalized to anyone in uniform—especially if that uniform resembles the one the mail carrier wears.

The United States Postal Service reports about three thousand bites a year, and educates both its carriers and the public on how to prevent dog attacks. In the best interest of dogs and mail carriers everywhere, dog owners are well advised to restrain or retrain their dogs to keep from adding to those bite statistics.

If you have the same mail carrier most days and get your mail through a slot in the door, we have a way to get your dog looking forward to the postal delivery. If your carrier's willing to cooperate, of course. Leave an airtight container of dog cookies just outside your door. Ask the carrier to drop a cookie through the slot along with the mail. It might take weeks, but eventually you are likely to see your dog sitting by the door slot, happily anticipating a sumptuous message from her favorite visitor.

Q: Is it true that barking dogs don't bite?

A: **Barking dogs can and do bite.** So will dogs who make no sound at all. The idea that a dog growls before biting is one you should not count on when dealing with any dog.

Q: Can dog lovers use some kind of Lassie LoJac to keep tabs on their pets?

A: The eight most common words heard by veterinarians from desperate pet owners are, "He never got out of the yard before!"

Hearing about a lost dog strikes fear into any pet lover, and for good reason. One out of every three pets is lost some time in the animal's life. Dogs may be startled into escaping because of fireworks or some other loud noise, or they may wander away after the repairman or gardener leaves a gate open. And when a disaster hits, many a pampered house dog finds himself on the streets for the first time, unprepared for life on the run.

Despite the many heartwarming stories we've all heard about dogs traveling hundreds of miles to find their way home, dogs do not come equipped with an internal homing device. Lost dogs are just as likely to be lost forever. If your dog goes AWOL, he is relying on you to find him. And that can be difficult, because no single system for identifying or tracking a stray dog is perfect.

ID tags are the first line of defense, and can be great for reuniting a frantic owner with a lost dog. But someone has to catch a stray dog to read the tag, and even so, tags and collars can fall off. Tattoos and microchips are a more permanent system of identification, but they have problems, too. For microchips to work, a dog must be found, caught and scanned with special equipment (assuming the chip is registered and the information is current) before the story ends happily ever after. Tattoos (usually done in the ear or on an inside flank) are not always found or understood.

So what about a "Lassie LoJac"? Not surprisingly, new GPS (global positioning system) and GSM (global system for mobile communications) technologies can give dog owners a way to track or contact a missing hound. Some clever manufacturers are already adapting these technologies to help Lassie go home, and more surely will follow.

Of course, nothing you put on or in your dog is guaranteed to protect him if he's loose or get him home once he's missing. That's why the best way to make sure your pet's safe is to be proactive rather than reactive. Good fences, self-closing gates and strong leashes will keep Rover from roaming.

That doesn't mean you should ignore tags, microchips,

tattoos and "Lassie LoJacs," because despite all good intentions and preparations, people and pets do become separated. Do what you can to manage a happy reunion, just in case.

Q: Does a wagging tail always mean a friendly dog?

A: *To get a read on a dog's attitude,* it's important to look at the whole dog. A dog who's up on her toes with her eyes focused in a hard stare and hackles raised may well have her tail up and wagging—but she is not a friendly dog.

A dog who's relaxed, smiling in a doggy grin and wagging her tail in a lower position is more likely to be friendly.

A nervous dog who may snap from fright may also be wagging her tail, but it's likely to be held lower.

Q: Why are some dogs so yappy?

A: **Why do some people seem** to have no ears and pie-holes that never shut? Dogs bark to express a variety of feelings: excitement, anxiety, boredom, territoriality, aggression, playfulness and hunger, to name a few. In addition, barking sessions can be triggered by certain conditions in the dog's environment. For example, a dog who barks a warning when strangers are near will bark constantly and frantically if one side of a fence separates his area in his yard from a well-traveled sidewalk. Likewise, an intelligent, high-energy dog who is neglected and bored in a lonely backyard may rid himself of that excess energy by indulging in barking sessions, day or night, that can last for hours.

Breed characteristics factor in, as well. Expecting an Arctic breed not to engage in an occasional howl, or a hound not to bay when he's on the trail of a squirrel or rabbit, is unrealistic. Some herding dogs drive livestock by nipping and barking at their heels, and their suburban relations many generations removed from the farm may still yap joyfully at the heels of the family's children at play.

In a way, we have no one to blame but ourselves for dogs barking—or at least, we can blame our ancestors. Adult wolves don't bark much, but in breeding early domestic dogs we valued the yapping that in wolves is the behavior of juveniles. The barking helped us to protect our property by sounding an alarm and letting intruders know a dog was on guard. So we kept and bred the dogs who liked to bark.

Unfortunately, in today's close living quarters, there's more to bark at—and neighbors closer in who don't appreciate the racket.

Q: Can a dog be trained not to bark?

A: **You can train a dog not to bark** by first training her to bark on command. Barking is normal for a dog, but you want to be able to put your finger on the "off" switch.

What do you do if you are not home to train or turn off the yapfest? A lot of problem barkers are healthy, active young dogs stuck alone outside without anything to do. A bored, lonely dog is going to find some way to fill the long hours, and barking is one of the choices. Slap an electronic collar on that dog and do nothing else to improve her life and she might take up destructive chewing instead. Not a good plan for anyone.

If you bring a barker into your life, start with training and exercise and you'll cut down a lot of the need to bark. You can reduce the yapping even more by removing cues that get your dog fired up. A dog who runs a fence line with a neighbor's dog, for example, won't bark so much if she's denied access to that part of the yard. Eliminate other bark triggers by keeping dogs indoors with a radio playing static (to muffle sound triggers such as other dogs barking in the distance).

Keep dogs who love the sound of their own voices away from front windows, or close the curtains to block visual cues. If the barking only occurs when the dog is alone, consult your veterinarian or a local behaviorist to determine if the constant yapping is a symptom of separation anxiety or hyperterritorial warnings. There are many, many reasons why a dog barks, so don't be fooled into thinking one size fits all.

If you've done everything you can and still find yourself with a dog who won't shut up, never scream at your dog. The dog will just think, "Cool! Now we're all barking." Dogs learn by imitation, so don't model what you don't want.

Many trainers recommend antibark collars that shoot a puff of citronella gas or just plain air when a dog pipes up. A barking dog finds the smell or sound or both annoying and distracting, and puts two and two together, resulting in less barking. But remember, this only works when you have given your dog all the exercise and stimulation she needs.

A recent study for the American Kennel Club to help promote greater responsibility by dog owners reveals that people who have dogs pretty much agree with people who don't about what makes troublesome dog owners: People who don't pick up after their dogs, and people who let their dogs bark or can't control them. If you recognize those characteristics in yourself, clean up your act. Picking up after your pet on walks is easy and would blunt a lot of criticism. Barking and out-of-control behavior are a little harder to tackle for many dog owners, but it's nothing that some time spent with a behaviorist or in an obedience class wouldn't help fix.

Q: Can a dog be trained to relieve herself on command?

A: Yes, and no. Dogs can certainly be taught a cue word that lets them know now's the right time to do the deed. Start with a dog you know needs to go, take her outside, say "go potty" and then follow up the deed with praise. Your dog will likely pick up on this routine quickly.

If the dog isn't getting the message and has some lapses, you might have to start her housetraining over from the beginning, as if she were a puppy. This means confining the dog in a portable kennel when she is not 100 percent supervised. (The reluctance many dogs have to soil their own resting area gives the dog a reason to "hold it.") Take the dog out directly to the designated toilet spot every few hours and repeat your preferred cue. (Make sure the cue you choose is something you will not be embarrassed to say in public, such as "get busy," "go potty" or even, "bombs away!") If the dog doesn't deliver, return her to the portable kennel and try again in twenty minutes or so. Reward deposits with a treat or, even better, a walk.

Keep up this routine until the dog has gone at least

five times in a row, in the designated area, on cue. This process is easy to teach to puppies, but can be more time-consuming in older dogs.

That said, you can't completely control the time and place where your dog goes, any more than you can completely control the timing of your own bathroom breaks. There will always be days when your pet's tummy doesn't agree with what she ate, or some other illness-related issue or change in routine (such as an increase in exercise and a long drink after) will make your pet's elimination routine less than entirely predictable.

Q: How long can a dog hold it before he has to pee?

A: **When you're housetraining puppies,** the general rule is that a puppy can hold it for as many hours as his age in months. In other words, a two-month-old puppy should be able to hold it for two hours, and a four-month-old puppy should be good for four hours.

In adult dogs, although many dogs routinely cross their legs for the same length of time as their owners' eight-hour workday (plus commute time) . . . really, a dog needs a potty break during the day every six hours or so. Some breeds, notably the toys, may not be able to hold it even that long. And all dogs lose bladder and bowel control as they age.

For tiny dogs kept indoors all day, one solution is a canine litter box. Larger dogs can make use of a dog door—if your home includes a securely fenced backyard. For any dog left home alone all day, having a dog walker, pet sitter or neighbor drop in while you're gone would be a kindness to both of you—since, if your dog cannot wait, you'll be cleaning up the mess!

The longest documented case of "holding it" is more than 36 hours, held by a Lhasa Apso. The veterinarian reported the dog was taken out to pee before closing Saturday, and the kennel person didn't show up until Sunday. Monday morning the cage was still dry, and the dog then urinated a prodigious amount outside. This is not normal or healthy, by the way.

Q: How do dogs trained to assist the vision-impaired know when the traffic light is green?

A: **Service dogs trained** to assist the vision-impaired don't know when the traffic signal changes. You may have read that dogs are color-blind—they're not, by the way—but the fact is that service dogs don't decide when to step off the curb. That's the job of their handlers. It's the dogs' job to decide if it's safe to proceed after the command is given to them, and that decision is made after assessing the potential hazards in the path ahead. If cars are crossing in front of the dog, the dog will not move forward.

Dogs trained to assist vision-impaired companions are a relative rarity among working dogs, because a big part of their training is learning when it's important to disobey. This is called "selective disobedience" or "intelligent disobedience," and is often considered the highest level of training.

Think about it: Most working dogs are trained to get some job done reliably, on command, every single time.

They're supposed to sniff out the drugs or bombs, bite the bad guy, find the missing person, round up the sheep or retrieve the bird. When a blind person tells a service dog what to do, the person often doesn't know what they're really asking because they can't see the hazards in front of them. The dog has to know when to disobey, and the owner has to support the dog's decisions.

It's a partnership built on respect and trust. Neither the dog nor the person is in total control at any time. Their lives depend on each other. Neither could cross the street safely without the other.

Q: Does the work search-and-rescue dogs do make them sad?

A: People make a mistake when they see a tired working dog and interpret the animal's demeanor as depression or grief. Depression suggests an awareness of the surroundings to the point where sadness is the result. It also suggests an understanding of death that dogs do not have.

If death depressed dogs, a dog might also get depressed when he sees a dead dog on the side of the road. He doesn't. To be blunt, death to a dog—or any predator—is often going to mean food. Why would that upset them?

Search-and-rescue work is physically and mentally exhausting to a dog. In addition to the dog's exhaustion, it's possible some dogs are reacting to the emotions of their handlers. Search-and-rescue work sometimes yields results that sadden a dog's human partner, and dogs read us so keenly that they can certainly pick up on that.

Q: Are Border Collies really the smartest dogs?

A: Want to pick a fight? Tell the owner of an Afghan Hound that her dog is dumb as a rock. And yet, that was the conclusion of Stanley Coren's bestselling book, *The Intelligence of Dogs,* which ranked most dog breeds based on how they performed on tests and in various canine sports.

At the top? The Border Collie, a dog considered so quick to learn and driven to perform that the brighter ones could probably do your taxes for you.

At the bottom. Well . . . you know—long of limb, silky of coat and poetry in motion. The Afghan Hound. But is the Afghan really the canine equivalent of the human "dumb blond"? It all depends on how you look at things.

Like many of the herding and sporting dogs at the top of the list, the Border Collie was developed to work with a human partner, maintaining constant contact and instantly obeying commands. As a result, you have a dog who learns quickly, in part because she's taking her cues from the humans around her.

But breeds were developed for different jobs, and some of those require working independently. Like all the sighthounds, the Afghan Hound was developed to run down prey in open fields. The breed's abilities in this area are without question. But this is a task that requires the dog to run far ahead of her human partner and make decisions on her own. She's well suited for this work, and it's not the Afghan Hound's fault that the job she was bred to do leaves her saying "huh?" when you try to teach her a complicated training routine.

We'll concede the point that when it comes to working out problems, learning new behaviors and performing with single-minded intensity, no breed can top the Border Collie. But be careful about dissing Afghan Hounds. They do their job very well, and look stylish while doing it. That's something we should all strive for!

WELCOME TO THE LAB-ORATORY!

Sirloin, our black Labrador Retriever, is the dumbest dog I've ever met.

Or so I think.

Beyond food and water, Sirloin has few basic needs. Not counting, of course, someone to endlessly throw toys for him to retrieve, someone to do a little Aladdin action on his belly, and someone to throw him an emotional biscuit every now and then. These emotional treats are delivered in the form of such syrupy, disjointed sentences as, "Gomer [that's one of his nicknames], youzzz is just the bestest boy in the world . . . and mommy loves you . . . yaazzzz she does."

Although his father was allegedly a runner-up National Field Trial Champion (anyone interested in buying the Brooklyn Bridge?), Sirloin could only place in the National Field Mouse Digging Championship. He'd also never cut it as a police dog, assistance dog, herding dog or drug detection dog. He's just too dumb.

Or is he?

Let me rethink this. He landed a cushy job and has never missed a day or night serving as the official doorman of Almost Heaven Ranch. He faithfully greets everyone at the door each time it opens and proudly escorts all departing visitors to the door, as well. Despite sleeping on the job about twenty hours of each day, he gets more rewards for less effort than any other worker on the ranch.

A typical day in the life of Sirloin consists of eating, sleeping, playing with his canine companions, Scooter and Lucky, chasing chipmunks he never catches and licking himself in hard-to-reach places—because he can.

Without fail, he can coerce anyone he meets into giving him extra treats with just one look from his dreamy, love-filled eyes, by scratching us with a paw, or by laying his head on our laps. Fur-get flunking obedience school; Sirloin has discovered a Universal Law of Dogdom: For every action (begging) there is an equal and opposite reaction (treats).

On second thought, Sirloin is no dummy. Behind that mask lies the best of both worlds; the heart of Ernest (and the clever antics of one of the Little Rascals), and the brain of Einstein.

—Dr. Marty Becker

Q: How fast is the fastest dog?

A: Dog speeds are somewhat controversial, because field conditions and distances, as well as methods of timing, vary considerably. Some dogs are timed by hand with a stopwatch, some digitally from a box start, and some by a car speedometer—the latter being notoriously inaccurate.

It's generally agreed that the fastest breed of dog is the Greyhound. And the fastest Greyhounds run at speeds of just under forty-two miles per hour—almost as fast as a thoroughbred racehorse.

These speedsters are notoriously quiet and could even be called lazy when they're not on the run—which is why various Greyhound adoption groups have chosen to market the dogs with the clever slogan, "Adopt a forty-mph couch potato."

Q: Do dogs really need a backyard to be happy?

A: **Some suburban dogs** with all the yard in the world aren't as lucky as some city dogs with no yard at all. That's because too many dog owners assume a dog is perfectly happy to spend her life mostly outside—alone. They forget that dogs are social animals, just as we are, and too much time alone can break their hearts.

It can also make them unruly and unsocialized. A dog who spends hours alone every day in the yard may be so crazy-happy to see somebody—anybody—that she will jump all over that person. With all that pent-up energy, eventually she can become difficult to train and control.

City dogs have their own challenges, of course, but spending quality time with their owners usually isn't one of them. For one thing, city dogs usually get lots of walks (unless they're small enough to use newspapers or a doggy litter box for a relief zone). And on those walks, there are plenty of wonderful smells and people and other dogs to greet. Of course, most enjoy some off-leash romping, but there are safe, fenced areas in most cities where the urban cool canine can stretch out and run.

Dogs are amazingly adaptable and resourceful animals. As long as they have good company, food, exercise, training and attention (and a good relationship with their veterinarian, of course), they can be happy in almost any environment where humans can be found. With or without a yard.

Q: Is doggy day care a good idea?

A: In recent years there's been an explosion in the number of doggie day care businesses—places where dogs are left for a day of play while their owners toil at work. Whether these businesses are right for your dog depends, of course, on your dog.

The dog who'd probably get the most out of the experience is one whose high-energy needs aren't being addressed by his owner, and who loves the dog park experience of playing with other friendly dogs.

Dogs who probably aren't meant for day care include those who are shy or aggressive around other dogs, are older and less active or who have other physical or emotional issues that make the experience stressful or unhappy for them and for the day care center's other customers.

Dogs who love day care really love it. Often they bound in to see their friends with an enthusiasm that may leave their owner asking, "What am I? Chopped liver?"

Q: Is it okay to let my dog drink salt water at the beach or slurp at the Muddy Puddle Cantina?

A: *To be honest,* it's going to be difficult to keep a swimming dog from taking in a certain amount of salt water. But you shouldn't encourage drinking, nor should you figure that drinking salt water will quench your dog's thirst.

Whenever you take your dog to a beach, be sure to pack lots of fresh water for drinking. And after your romp, make sure you hose your dog down with clean, fresh water to get off all the salt and sand.

Drinking from puddles, ponds and lakes is also not a great idea. Standing water of any kind is often a teeming metropolis of organisms that are just waiting to colonize any creature foolish enough to stick in a tongue. If the water isn't clean and fresh enough for you, it's not good enough for your dog, either. And while you might not end up at the veterinary emergency clinic with a sick dog, you might end up on your hands and knees cleaning up vomiting or diarrhea.

Q: How far and how high can a dog jump?

A: A few years ago the sport of dock diving began in earnest. To compete, dogs run the length of a raised dock and jump into the air after a thrown object. Safe landings are provided by a long, narrow swimming pool, which is probably why many of the dogs who compete in the sport are dogs bred to work in water.

A long-legged speedster such as a Greyhound may be able to get enough takeoff speed to shatter any record set by a Labrador Retriever, but you're just not going to find that many Greyhounds who fancy the idea of jumping off a dock into a pool.

Anyway, you go with the records you have. The dominant organization in the sport is a group called Dock Dogs, and they have records both for distance and height (the latter is called Big Air competition). While the records will surely be broken in this relatively young sport, as of this writing the height record is almost seven feet and the distance record stands at a tick over twenty-eight feet, or almost the height of a three-story building.

Q: Why don't retrievers eat the birds instead of bringing them back to the hunter?

A: "Selective breeding" is the short answer. We humans have spent centuries developing dogs who will help us hunt without helping themselves to what we've hunted. So retrievers maintain their desire to retrieve but inhibit their interest in eating the quarry.

The perfect hunting retriever is a dog who's "birdy" (interested in finding and retrieving birds), has "drive" (is willing to work hard in all conditions), and has a "soft mouth" (will hold the bird without crushing it).

In the old days, when people hunted for food rather than sport, if a hunting dog ate or even crunched down on the bird, it wouldn't be fit for the dinner table. In other words, that dog did not earn his keep, and even took food off the table. He (or she) would certainly not be bred, because nobody wanted that trait passed on to the next generation.

A dog who was so timid that he would not try to find downed prey was not much use either. As a practical consideration, those hunting dogs who were chosen to be bred—and still are, to this day—are those with the drive and desire to find a downed bird and the bite inhibition to deliver it to the hunter with nary a ruffled feather.

Q: How can sled dogs survive sleeping in snowbanks?

A: **If you had a coat like a sled dog's,** you'd be able to sleep in snowbanks, too. Their coats provide good insulation, especially if you add in the insulating factor of the snow itself. Think igloos!

Dog-sledding participants say they have animals whose coats are so remarkably thick and provide such excellent insulation that snow on top of the fur doesn't melt from the dog's body heat. They also say some of their dogs prefer to sit out in the open on bitter-cold days, even when warm shelters are available.

Q: Who decides if and when Labradoodles and Puggles will get to compete at dog shows?

A: It depends on who is putting on the dog show. There are lots of fun matches, 4-H shows and county fairs where any dog can compete. But if you're talking about the fancy shows, like the Westminster Kennel Club dog show, the American Kennel Club (AKC) does the deciding. And if you're hoping to see mixed breeds at AKC shows, we advise you not to hold your breath.

Like all AKC-sanctioned dog shows, Westminster is for AKC-registered purebreds only, and it's sure to remain so, no matter how popular the current trend of mixed breeds with cute names.

People who love their Puggles (Pug-Beagles) and Labradoodles (Labrador Retriever-Poodles) may call them breeds, but the AKC sees it differently. To be a pure breed, dogs of that breed must be mated to other dogs of the exact same breed. So a Pug mated to a Pug produces pure Pug puppies. Simple!

By their very definition, the so-called "designer dogs" have parents of two different breeds. In the AKC's eyes, that makes them crossbreeds; definitely ineligible for any AKC competition—not only dog shows, but also agility and obedience trials, hunt tests and all the rest.

Most breeds did start as some kind of mix, because people wanted to combine some traits of one breed with the qualities of another to get just the dog they wanted. Eventually, those traits became fixed, which means that when dogs with the same mix were bred to one another, the resulting puppies looked and behaved just like their parents. That's how dogs become purebred.

As long as a Labradoodle is a Poodle crossed with a Labrador Retriever, the resulting offspring will vary in their traits—for example, some will have Poodle coats and some will have Labrador coats—because it's a roll of the genetic dice which breed traits will be inherited from each parent. Those dogs will never be considered purebreds by the AKC, and the various resulting combinations will not be considered a breed.

Is there any hope for the Labradoodle lover who dreams of a Westminster Best in Show? If these dogs get to a point where they're the product of "pure" breeding—Labradoodles bred to Labradoodles instead of Labradors bred to Poodles—then it's possible a breed club could seek AKC recognition. To get it, a breed has to have a widespread geographical following, a certain minimum number of dogs, a national parent club, a breed standard (which describes the ideal characteristics of the breed) and a good record of its breedings for several generations.

Q: Is it true that some dogs have hair that grows into dreadlocks?

A: The two breeds most people think of when it comes to dreadlocks (dog breeders call them "cords") are the Komondor and the Puli. The hair of the Poodle will also grow into cords if allowed, and very rarely a corded Poodle is seen on the dog show circuit.

The hair on these dogs has a natural tendency to mat and twist as the dog matures. Fanciers shape growing fur into cords and protect the cords like treasures, which they are: More than one or two missing cords on a show dog may mean the end of a career. It's not uncommon for a top show dog to have cords that brush the floor.

Maintaining a dog in cords is one of the most difficult tasks in the dog show world. It takes days to prepare a dog for the show ring, gently soaping, rinsing and wringing a few cords at a time—work similar to hand-washing an expensive, delicate (and giant!) sweater. A particularly dirty dog will need to have the whole job repeated until the cords are all the same color. To make things even more difficult, Pulis come in several colors, including white, and all Komondors should be white—or at least off-white.

Because the wet cords are prone to mildew, the freshly washed dogs are put in raised drying cages with fans blowing on them from all directions. A corded dog left to dry naturally may stay wet for several days.

When a corded dog's show career ends, the floor-length cords are usually cut off. A few years ago, one top Komondor was retired and shaved down—relieving him of almost 2,700 individual cords and 15 pounds of hair overall.

Q: Are show Poodles embarrassed to look like that?

A: *The Poodle's overdone "do"* was originally developed for practical reasons. The puffs of hair around the joints and the vital organs were left in place to protect a dog who was working as a hunting retriever in cold water. The rest of the hair was shaved to make it easier for the dog to swim. Even the pompom on the tail had a purpose: supposedly, to make it easier to spot the dog in tall grass.

In today's show rings, the Poodle's polish is definitely exaggerated. But Poodles take it all in stride, perhaps because they're athletic, intelligent dogs with enough self-confidence to not care what anyone thinks.

QUIT PICKING ON POODLES!

Long maligned as an effeminate dandy, the Poodle has been the butt of jokes for generations, probably ever since the first person put a fancy haircut on what had been a hardworking hunting dog. But the soul of the Poodle is still there, under everything that's ever been done to the hair.

And oh, there has been a lot done! The curly coat of the Poodle has been cut in every imaginable way, dyed in every possible color, and (less commonly) even been left alone to work its way into floor-length cords that make the dog look like a French Rastafarian.

As if all that humiliation weren't enough, people who keep Poodles seem to share a higher-than-average desire to dress up their pups in all kinds of getups, from faux leopard-skin jackets and pearl collars to leather biker jackets with leashes to match.

But looks alone shouldn't define a dog, and that's surely true with the Poodle. I got a letter recently from someone who wanted me to recommend a breed for her family. She wanted a dog who is relatively clean and low-shedding, smart, playful and easy to train. And then she wrote this: "My husband will go with anything except a Poodle."

How fair is that? And how sensible, when a Poodle fits that family's requirements perfectly? Instead of crossing the Poodle off the list, I suggested the reader consider what a Poodle is really like. Anyone who does so will find a lot to appreciate.

The Poodle is a smart dog—one of the smartest by most any measure. Poodles learn quickly and love to show off what they know. They make novice trainers look expert and expert trainers look brilliant. And they make fools out of the poor owners who don't realize just how smart a dog they have.

The Poodle is a friendly dog. Poodles have an innate sense of cheerful confidence and a firm belief that everyone should be entitled to the pleasure of their company. They are the consummate companions.

The Poodle is a hardworking dog. Some Poodle fanciers are trying to restore the breed to its working heritage. Poodles excel in obedience and agility, naturally, but a few are even showing up in hunting circles. Poodles as sled dogs? That, too, has happened. They love to have a job to do.

Most of all, the Poodle is a dog with a great sense of humor, which is important to a breed that has been through all this one has. Poodles will laugh at you, but they are really happier to laugh with you, genial souls that they are. And they even seem able to laugh at themselves.

A few years back, I was at the Westminster Kennel Club dog show, standing next to a big Standard Poodle who was waiting to go into the ring for the Best in Show competition. The poor fellow's fanny had been shaved in a way that no living thing should have to endure, and I'm sure his sperm count fell with every draft of cool air. And yet, as the dog and I briefly made eye contact, he cracked his mouth in a happy smile, shook his well-coiffed head and winked.

As I stood there gaping (wondering, did I really see that?), the dog turned and went into the ring with his handler, Poodle pride in every high step. How could you not love a dog like that?

—Gina Spadafori

Q: Are some breeds really hypoallergenic?

A: All dogs have the potential to cause misery in allergy sufferers, no matter what the breed or mix, or the hair type—or lack thereof.

The breeds that are reputed to be preferred for allergy sufferers are those with Poodle-like coats. The list includes Poodles, of course, but also Maltese, Bichons Frises and some doodle-oodle mixes (Labradoodles, Cockapoos and so on). Some people also believe that dogs with little or no hair, like the Chinese Crested, are better choices for allergy sufferers.

The problem with the fur theory is that it's not the fur that causes the problems. Allergies are caused by a substance found in the sebaceous glands in a dog's skin. This sneeze-and-wheeze-inducing substance clings to the dog's skin and hair and ends up everywhere as the dog moves around the house. There is no escape for people with allergies. Yes, you can get a dog without hair, but you can't get one without skin. If you really want a hypoallergenic pet, think about a reptile, or maybe a fish.

(Not birds, because feathers and feather dust will get you!)

That said, some breeds seem to be better tolerated by some people with allergies, but reactions vary from person to person and dog to dog. The American Kennel Club suggests fifteen breeds that may be easier on allergy sufferers: the Bedlington Terrier, Bichon Frise, Chinese Crested, Irish Water Spaniel, Kerry Blue Terrier, Maltese, all three sizes of Poodle, Portuguese Water Dog, all three sizes of Schnauzer, Soft-Coated Wheaten Terrier and Xoloitzcuintli. (We didn't make that last one up! The Xolo is a breed of hairless dog native to Mexico.)

In general, smaller dogs seem to be less of a problem than larger ones, but that's because smaller dogs put out smaller amounts of allergen. Bathing or even rinsing your dog frequently can help, as can keeping pets out of your bedroom so you can have allergy-free sleep.

What about that other dog-allergy-related urban myth, that Chihuahuas can cure asthma? The sound you hear is a thousand allergists laughing.

Q: Are any breeds of dogs "made in America"?

A: **According to the American Kennel Club,** breeds developed in the United States include the Alaskan Malamute, American Eskimo Dog, American Foxhound, American Water Spaniel, American Staffordshire Terrier, Australian Shepherd, Black and Tan Coonhound, Boston Terrier, Chesapeake Bay Retriever, Plott Hound and Toy Fox Terrier. (You read that right: The Australian Shepherd in an American dog.)

There are other American breeds that are not recognized by the AKC, including the Boykin Spaniel, various Coonhounds and the Catahoula Leopard Dog.

Q: Final question: Do you guys ever get tired of giving advice to pet lovers every day of your lives until the end of time?

A: **Of course not!** It's either do this or get real jobs. Not to mention, how many jobs can you have in this world where every single day you can make someone's life a little better, just by sharing your love of animals and your hard-earned knowledge of how to make living with them easier?

Not many, huh? Truth to tell, we consider ourselves lucky, and more than a little bit blessed.

And that, as they say, is our final answer.

Acknowledgments

This book, and its feline companion volume, would not have been possible without the generosity of the many top veterinarians, trainers, breeders and other experts who were gracious and generous in providing their expertise. These professionals have written textbooks, published bestsellers and are the folks who people crowd into rooms to hear giving keynotes at major meetings. It's exciting and inspiring to us to know and be able to share ideas with such an outstanding group of professionals—brilliant and caring people who have dedicated their careers to improving the lives of pets and the people who love them.

We both owe so much to Marty's colleague, Dr. Rolan Tripp of *AnimalBehavior.net,* and his wife, Susan, for their keen and expert eyes on this project, their injections of creativity, and their help in making everything good even better.

Our gratitude also goes out to all the veterinarians who helped us. We especially want to thank Dr. Bonnie Beaver; Dr. Mark Bekoff, professor of ecology and evolutionary biology at the University of Colorado; Dr. Jan Bellows of Pembroke Pines, Florida; Dr. Pierre S. Bichsel of Michigan Veterinary Specialists near Detroit; Dr. Tony Buffington, professor of veterinary clinical sciences, the Ohio State University; Dr. Gilbert Burns, associate professor of anatomy at Washington State University College of Veterinary Medicine; Dr. Samuel Vainisi, Eye Care for Animals; Dr. Nicholas Dodman, head of the Animal Behavior Department at the Cummings School of Veterinary Medicine at Tufts University; Dr. Andrea Fascetti, veterinary nutritionist, UC Davis School of Veterinary Medicine; Dr. Duncan Ferguson, professor of veterinary medicine at the University of Georgia; Dr. Peter J. Ihrke, professor of dermatology at the University of California, Davis, School of Veterinary Medicine; Dr. Kit Kampschmidt of Brittmoore Animal Hospital in Houston, Texas; Dr. J. Veronika Kiklevich of Dr. K's Veterinary Dental Services in San Antonio, Texas; Dr. Bonnie Lefbom of Chesapeake Veterinary Cardiology Associates in Virginia; Dr. Karol Mathews, Ontario Veterinary College, University of Guelph; Dr. Fred Metzger of Metzger Animal Hospital in State College, Pennsylvania; O. Lynne Nelson, assistant professor at Washington State University College of Veterinary Medicine; Dr. Stu Nelson, chief veterinarian for the Iditarod; Dr. Paul Pion of the Veterinary Information Network and VeterinaryPartner.com; Dr. Narda Robinson, chief of complementary medicine at Colorado State University-Veterinary Medical Center; Drs. Karen Padgett and Phil Roudebush of Hill's Pet Nutrition; Dr. Jeff Werber of Century Veterinary Group in Los Angeles; and Dr. Sandy Wright, diplomate, American College of Veterinary Internal Medicine.

We also want to thank Dr. Harold Nelson of the National Jewish Medical and Research Center and Temple University's Dr. Ronald Baenninger. Everything we know about fleas we owe to Dr. Michael Dryden, a professor of veterinary parasitology at Kansas State University's College of Veterinary Medicine. (Dr. Dryden has license plates that read "Dr Flea"—we love it!)

We could not have managed without the collected wisdom of Dr. Roger Abrantes, author of *The Evolution of Canine Social Behavior*; Darlene Arden, author of *Small Dogs, Big Hearts*; sled-dog racer and author Margaret Bonham; Susan Bulanda, author of *Ready: The Training of the Search and Rescue Dog*; Jane Brackman, former executive director of Guide Dogs of America and owner of Sirius Press; Dr. Stanley Coren, author of *The Intelligence of Dogs*; Westminster Kennel Club spokesman David Frei; Suzanne Hetts of Animal Behavior Associates in Littleton, Colorado; Larry Lachman, animal behavior consultant and author of *Dogs on the Couch*; top dog trainers and bestselling authors Brian Kilcommons, Liz Palika and Pat Miller; Chris Walkowicz, a dog show judge, author and breeder of many generations of champion Bearded Collies and German Shepherds; and retriever trainer, breeder and hunt test judge Mary Young.

On a more personal level, we simply cannot do what we do without the support of our family and friends.

For Marty, two-legged family includes his beloved wife, Teresa (a gifted writer in her own right), daughter, Mikkel and son, Lex. Not to mention the four-legged family members—dogs, cats and horses—on the Becker family's Almost Heaven Ranch in northern Idaho. Worthy of special recognition is his colleague, friend and mentor, Dr. Scott Campbell, the founder, CEO and chairman of the board of Banfield, the Pet Hospital.

For Gina, two-legged family starts with her brother Joe, who is also one of her very best friends. Always, too, there's support of her parents, Louise and Nino, fifty-two years married and still going strong, and her brother Pete, his wife, Sally and their bright and talented children, Kate and Steven. This book would not have been possible without the help of Gina's community of friends, colleagues and pet lovers, especially Dr. Signe Beebe, Judithanne Bloom, Melinie DiLuck, Jan Haag, Sonia Hansen, Don Linville, Christie Keith, Scott Mackey, John McDonald, Greg Melvin, Morgan Ong, Dr. Bill Porte, Dick Schmidt, Monica Siewert and Mary Young. And of course, the pet residents of the Northern California home Gina is now calling the Almost Crazy Ranch.

Thanks from us both to the folks at Health Communications, Inc., especially Peter Vegso, who saw the promise of this book and its feline companion volume and gave us the go-ahead to write together and have a great time doing so. We'd also like to note in appreciation and heartfelt respect the work of our project editor, Allison Janse and our copy editor, Beth Adelman.

—Dr. Marty Becker, drmartybecker.com

—Gina Spadafori, petconnection.com

Do you have a question?

We know you have more than 101 questions about your dog! So we're already planning another book to answer even more of your questions.

Would you like your question answered in the next book? Drop us a line at *askaboutpets@gmail.com*, or contact us through our Web sites. We're looking forward to your questions.

About the Authors

Dr. Marty Becker

As a veterinarian, media personality, author and educator, Dr. Marty Becker has become known as the "best-loved family doctor for pets."

Marty is the popular veterinary contributor to ABC-TV's *Good Morning, America.* He is also the author of two highly regarded newspaper columns distributed by the McClatchy-Tribune Information Services (formerly Knight Ridder Tribune). In association with the American Animal Hospital Association, Marty hosts a nationally syndicated radio program, *Top Vets Talk Pets,* on the Health Radio Network. He has appeared on Animal Planet, and is a frequent guest on national network and cable television, and radio shows.

Marty is an adjunct professor at both his alma mater, the Washington State University College of Veterinary Medicine, and at the Colorado State University College of

Veterinary Medicine. Additionally, he has lectured at every veterinary school in the United States, and been named Companion Animal Veterinarian of the Year by the Delta Society and the American Veterinary Medical Association.

Marty is coauthor of the fastest-selling pet book in history, *Chicken Soup for the Pet Lover's Soul,* and is either sole author or coauthor of other top-selling books, including other animal books in the *Chicken Soup* line, *The Healing Power of Pets: Harnessing the Amazing Ability of Pets to Make and Keep People Happy and Healthy*, and *Fitness Unleashed: A Dog and Owner's Guide to Losing Weight and Gaining Health Together!*

Marty devotes his life to his family, which includes his beloved wife, Teresa, daughter, Mikkel and son, Lex, along with all the furry family members on the Beckers' Almost Heaven Ranch in northern Idaho.

Gina Spadafori

Gina Spadafori has been blessed with the opportunity to combine two of her dearest loves—animals and words—into a career writing about animals. Since 1984, she has written an award-winning weekly column on pets and their care, which now appears in newspapers across the United States and Canada through the Universal Press Syndicate.

Gina has served on the boards of directors of both the Cat Writers Association and the Dog Writers Association of America. She has won the DWAA's Maxwell Medallion for the best newspaper column, and her column has also been honored with a certificate of excellence by the CWA. The first edition of her top-selling book *Dogs For Dummies* was given the President's Award for the best writing on dogs and the Maxwell Medallion for the best general reference work, both by the DWAA.

Along with coauthor Dr. Paul D. Pion, a top veterinary cardiologist, she was given the CWA's awards for the best work on feline nutrition, best work on feline behavior, and best work on responsible cat care for the top-selling *Cats For Dummies*. The book was also named one of the one hundred best feline moments in the twentieth century by *Cat Fancy* magazine. With internationally recognized avian specialist Dr. Brian L. Speer, Gina has also written *Birds For Dummies*, one of the bestselling books on pet birds ever written. Her books have been translated into many languages, including French, Serbian, Danish, Japanese and Russian.

Gina has also headed one of the first and largest online pet care sites, the Pet Care Forum, America Online's founding source of pet care information.

Gina lives in northern California in a decidedly multi-species home.

About the Cover Doggie

Tucker

Tucker is a Terrier mix, mostly Wheaten Terrier, approximately seven to eight years old, who was a rescue dog at the Amanda Foundation in Beverly Hills, California. "Amanda" is Latin for worthy of love, and Tucker surely is. He loves to take walks, play fetch and catch cookie treats. He is actually in training with a pet talent agency to try his hand (ahem, paw) at Hollywood and some day walk the red carpet.

About the Amanda Foundation

The Amanda Foundation has been finding loving homes for dogs and cats for over thirty years. For more information, contact: *www.amandafoundation.org*.

The ideal gift for any pet lover.

Code #6129 • $7.95

Code #6137 • $7.95

To order direct: Telephone (800) 441-5569 • www.hcibooks.com
Prices do not include shipping and handling. Your response code is BKS.